# Motivating Without Money

**CASHLESS WAYS to**

**Stimulate Maximum Results,**

**Raise Morale, and Lower Turnover**

**With Your Telephone Sales and**

**Service Professionals**

# Dave Worman

**Business By Phone** Inc.

13254 Stevens St., Omaha, NE 68137   402-895-9399   Fax: 402-896-3353
www.businessbyphone.com

**Motivating Without Money**
*CASHLESS Ways to Stimulate Maximum Results,*
*Raise Morale, and Lower Turnover With Your*
*Telephone Sales and Service Professionals*
By Dave Worman

**Published By:**
Business By Phone Inc.
13254 Stevens St.
Omaha, NE 68137.
(402)895-9399
Fax:(402)896-3353
E-mail arts@businessbyphone.com
http://www.businessbyphone.com

*Cover design by George Foster, Foster & Foster, Fairfield, IA*
*Layout by Shepley Hanson, Bluebird Graphics, Fairfield, IA*
*Editing by Patricia Jacobs Hufnagel, Writing to Go, Fairfield, IA*

**ISBN 1-881081-10-9**

# Dedicated to...

Those who truly sacrificed to make this book a reality, my four best friends in the world, my family. My loving wife Kathy, my daughters Michelle and Jackie, and my son Danny... thank you for giving me the mental, physical, and spiritual strength, the endless encouragement and the unconditional support to pursue my passion for this project. I love you.

**SPECIAL THANKS TO...**

Art Sobczak. My thanks to you for your aggressive persistence for me to take on this challenge and the sincere encouragement that can only come from a true friend.

All of you, my colleagues throughout the world that have joined me for many years, working endlessly to bring pride, respectability, and abundant success to this fabulous industry of ours.

# Motivating Without Money

## TABLE OF CONTENTS

# Foreword

Many people asked me why in the world I would try to write another book in the midst of an already crazy schedule. My answer was simple: for you. My love for the industry of business-by-phone is no secret. Those of you that have read my first book *Motivating with Sales Contests* or have attended my presentations are well aware of my belief in the importance of keeping employees motivated and especially my passion for using non-monetary motivation. I want you, my fellow telesales leaders, to experience some of the same managerial highs as I have while avoiding some of the leadership lows that could possibly be waiting for you right around the corner. Over the years, telesales directors, managers and supervisors from around the globe have asked me to gather the information on the subject of non-monetary motivation from my articles, interviews, presentations and seminars and present them in a book. And now I'm pleased to tell you, here it is.

Each of the following 17 chapters offers a guaranteed way to help you improve your employee performance and also reduce turnover. And none of these methods involves giving out cash, extra commissions, bonus plans or raises. That's right, *non-monetary motivation*. And I did say *guaranteed*. Since life has so few guarantees let's note for the record that this would definitely be one of them.

Having experienced the same managerial frustrations, setbacks and mistakes that many of you go through everyday, I have developed a formula based on proven motivational methods that stimulates more energy, enthusiasm and productivity in your employees. Granted, this formula also contains a mix of creative, unusual and what some may consider wacky ideas. But guess what? The formula works. And this formula in turn produces happier employees who enjoy greater success and ultimately more job loyalty.

Just like you, I deal with the painful reality that our budgets for additional incentives, bonuses and merit increases are certainly not on the rise. In fact, the common theme in business today is "maximum results at minimum cost." And this is no passing trend. It's here to stay. You know the terms; expectations are high and rising while the budget stays the same or in some cases gets reduced or eliminated. Well, don't panic because your world doesn't have to end. Not even close. As you take some of the ideas in this book that have worked so well for me and try using them in your own area, you could find yourself headed for better times than you've ever seen in your work environment. Remember that knowledge doesn't help you if you don't use it. The application of knowledge is what makes it powerful. Well, get ready to apply. And now sit back and enjoy because my dear colleagues—to quote the famous old beer commercial, "This one's for you."

Have Fun!
Dave

# Introduction

I wrote this book to save managers and supervisors in tele-marketing and telesales from doing 'hard time.' Hard time? Yes. As a former inmate, let me ask you if you're guilty of committing the same motivational crime I've been convicted of in the past. I'm not talking about the small management mis-demeanors we all commit from time to time as leaders. I mean the big one, the grand salami, and the ultimate felony: buying the theory that greater compensation means happier employ-ees. The theory that commissions, bonuses or raises make employees more positive or somehow better. I'm betting you're guilty, no jury necessary. You've committed and are continuing to commit motivational murder in the first degree. There, I've said it. It's hard for me to talk about it, to relive my dark past, to bring back the awful memories of unsuccessful and unhap-py time in a professional 'prison' environment. But my life of crime is behind me, a thing of the past. How about you?

If you're currently doing 'hard time' for motivational mur-der, this book can set you up for immediate parole and a hap-pier, more productive life on the 'outside.' And I hope many man-agers out there in the premeditative stages will use this book to avoid this felony that seems to be sweeping our industry. You've heard the statistics before, like every 30 seconds a car is stolen in New York? Well that's what's happening in our industry all over the world and all too often.

The belief and practice that money is the best or the only motivator will cost you valuable time, revenue, income, personal and corporate goals, employees, and, if you're not careful, your own job. And if you're like me, you're already under enough pressure as a leader for increasing productivity on a decreas-ing budget, right? You know what I'm talking about. While our departmental, divisional and corporate budgets are shrinking (dramatically in some cases), you and I are expected to meet aggressive performance goals and objectives, show maximum success, reduce turnover and keep employees happy, right? It makes you want to go out and play in the traffic, doesn't it? Well, lucky for all of us, there's no need to play in the street.

In this book, I will share what I know to be the 17 secret steps to maximum motivation that have nothing to do with raises, bonus checks or handing out $20 bills. That's right! These 17 proven steps will dramatically and immediately improve attitude and morale, increase productivity, reduce turnover and ultimately build a happier, healthier environment. It may sound too good to be true, but it works. And I'm not suggesting you hire David Copperfield as a consultant. There's no magic required. But I haven't mentioned the one crucial factor, **you**. According to Webster, motivation is "something from within that prompts or incites an action." If motivation comes from within then it's not your job to *motivate* other people. In fact—no offense—you can't. Our job as leaders is to create and maintain an environment where people will be *self-motivated*. And that's what these 17 chapters will do, as long as you're willing to put this information to use. Otherwise this book will only succeed in taking up shelf space. And gathering dust.

If you've seen my presentations and seminars at national and international conferences or used my services at your company, you've already sampled my intense belief and enthusiasm regarding these 17 steps to non-monetary motivation. And for those of you I haven't met in my travels, I look forward to that possibility in the future. But for all of you, I hope this book will provide an exciting journey, and that you will share in the burning enthusiasm that is renewed in me with each word I write.

### An Invitation

As you take ideas from this book and try them out in your

work environment, please share your results. I would love to hear your success stories. And as always I am available to aid companies in the design, creation and implementation of motivational programs for telemarketing and telesales environments. For consultation or a private seminar, please call me at 800-998-8496 ext. 4200 or at home at 815-434-6579, or email me at DWorman@Reliable.com.

## Final Thoughts

Finding creative ways to build and maintain a positive, productive environment in our industry is difficult enough. To achieve this without using dollars and cents is a monumental task. Creative motivation is a must. After many seminars on this very topic and hundreds of private presentations, it is clear that there is a huge demand for imaginative ways to keep the people in our industry positive and productive. It is important to understand that the 17 ideas that fill the following chapters are not theoretical and do not fall into the category of "throw enough stuff against the wall and some of it will stick," or "try them, who knows, they might work." *They all work.* They have always worked and they will continue to work. I base this on my own experience and on that of many people who have called me with exciting stories following a seminar or my visit to their company. Each one of these recommended steps used individually or in combination with one another has proved successful. And while some of the ideas may not seem revolutionary or may sound like "Telemarketing 101," ask yourself, "Have I been doing this?" or "Have I considered all the ways I could improve my environment by doing this?" And what makes us think we're ever beyond using basics and fundamentals? How many times have you heard the professionals say, "To get out of this slump, we need to get back to basics," or "In order to keep winning we must concentrate on the fundamentals." Basics and fundamentals never lose their value. We just forget to exercise them.

While some ideas may be new for you, I encourage you not to get lost in the paradigm that says, "We'll just keep doing what we've always done." I say, "Go for it, try something new. Remember that if you do what you've always done, you'll get what you've always gotten. Anyway, it's what we learn after we know it all that counts, right?

And here's one last motivator for you. You will find your people having more fun on the job than ever before. Did I say FUN? You bet I did and what's wrong with that? I'll tell you what's wrong with that. Nothing. I don't condone running a circus type of environment where goofing-off prevails over productivity, but a little fun and laughter make for happier employees which usually means lower turnover and greater success. I'm reminded of one of my former positions (names and company unnecessary) where we received a memo from a vice-president stating (among other things), "There will be no laughing in this division, ever!" What is that? I had to hide in a nearby office because I was afraid I'd get in trouble for laughing at the memo!

Get with the program, folks. A happy employee is a far more productive employee. And isn't that what you want? Ralph Waldo Emerson once said, "Nothing great was ever achieved without enthusiasm." How right he was. Buckle your seat belt and enjoy the ride.

# The Essential Compensation Plan

**D**on't get me wrong. I understand the power of the almighty dollar and the need to keep up with the rising cost of living. Cash will always be a major factor in employee motivation and a solid compensation plan is absolutely critical to attract and keep GOOD personnel. But the point to remember is that money is not the only answer and in many cases is not even the best solution for keeping your employees motivated.

Think about the tens of thousands of bonus and commission checks that get cashed, spent and forgotten. Grocery stores, gasoline stations and monthly bills are among the necessary interference that keep employees from remembering or appreciating what they worked so hard to achieve. Does this happen to you? It happened to me and that's why I highly recommend a change. As an alternative to cash for your bonus and commission structures, I strongly encourage you to implement **a catalog point system.** "What is that?" you ask. "Will it work?" Wake up, you guys, and put out the fire. Cash commissions and bonuses are burning a hole in your employees' pockets. Close your eyes and picture yourself waiting to receive your commission or bonus so you can fill up the car with gas and pay some of those bills at home we just talked about. Doesn't that sound exciting? Now, close your eyes again and picture yourself waiting to receive that same commission or bonus so you can choose from a gift catalog offering everything from clothing to televisions, tools to vacation travel and everything in between. Now which sounds more appealing?

Haven't we all looked through catalogs, mentally choosing things we couldn't afford? The catalog point system makes these dreams come true. That's why you need to save yourself from getting caught in the cash-incentive paradigm. The catalog incentive program spurs an epidemic of enthusiasm. I have used this exciting cash alternative with great success in my own environments since 1989 and now I strongly recommend it at conference and seminar presentations and to companies across North America during consulting assignments.

## What is a catalog/point
## system and why does it work?

One of the many benefits of this system is simplicity. Implementation requires very little cost, time and energy. Your commission/bonus structure remains exactly where it is now. The incentive company will provide you with all program materials such as catalogs, order forms and blank checks. Instead of cash, commission/bonus dollars are now equivalent to points.

EXAMPLE: 2 points = 1 cent or 5000 points = $25.00

Calculate each commission/bonus accordingly and distribute 'point' checks to your employees instead of cash.

Employees can choose to order from the catalog each time they receive a check, or accumulate points for more expensive gifts. The employee then fills out an order form and sends it in with the required number of points and the catalog company sends the gift. In my experience most people will try to accumulate points long term to win substantial items such as camcorders, televisions or even vacation trips. This accumulation option is beneficial to you, the manager, in various ways. First, it provides long-term motivation for the employee to earn enough points for their dream gifts. This special motivation is not visible when an employee is burning their commission every month or quarter on bills, gas and groceries. Second, there is huge gratification when the employee finally reaches the goal and orders the gift he's been working for. And third, and important to many of you, it reduces turnover.

That's right, you didn't just read a typo, this system reduces turnover. How? It's simple. When an employee gets cash commission/bonus on a monthly basis, it's easy to quit his (her) job at any time. There isn't much to lose. And habitually, you as manager get pulled into that time-consuming revolving door of recruiting, hiring and training. Employees on a catalog/point system, however, are less likely to quit suddenly when they still need points for their dream gifts. On this system, they generally stay longer. And once they're involved in the excitement of receiving their gifts they become even more likely to stay.

The stimulation attached to these gifts is everlasting. Every time they look at it or use it they remember their achievement and the manager and company that made it possible.

## Choosing the right incentive awards company

Selecting the catalog incentive company to work with is your first step and the most important decision you will face during the process of implementing your new plan. After dealing with exorbitant prices, delivery problems and poor customer service, I researched this industry extensively until I found the company I wanted to work with myself and also promote during presentations and private consulting. What a difference it made to find the 'right' company! Allow some of my bloodshed to pay off for you. First of all, many of these companies mark up the catalog prices 40 to 60 percent to cover middleman expenses. This will end up costing you more budget dollars and it will ultimately generate less interest with your people when they quickly realize the ridiculous number of points it takes to choose a decent item. Secondly, many of the catalogs are overwhelmingly filled with too many variations of too many gifts. A catalog displaying just three to five variations of many gift ideas is not only an adequate amount to choose from, it's far less expensive for the catalog company to produce. Think about it, why should you pay more because a company decided to put together a catalog so large that they have to cover that expense by climbing into your pocket? And do you want to work with a catalog that is so big you need an 'engine hoist' to lift it up on the desk? Not me.

It is also a benefit if the company you choose is a complete incentive company that can recommend ideas for your catalog/point program as well as other suggestions for incentive and awards programs.

When you get ready to start, or if my previous nightmares sound familiar because you're currently working with an unsatisfactory incentive company, **Louis Breeden, Inc.** is your answer. Located in Cincinnati, Ohio, Louis Breeden Promotions is a full-service advertising specialty company. He carries an unlimited supply of specialty and promotional products including pens, mugs, clocks, a variety of apparel, name-brand watches, electronics and outdoor products that can all be imprinted with your company name and logo if you choose. Breeden offers full-service incentive ideas and award programs including a catalog point system. If you're thinking, "Louis Breeden, where do I know that name from?" you're right. Louis Breeden is the former NFL all-pro corner back for the Cincinnati Bengals. Louis and I have been good friends since I met him in 1981 when I was Public Relations manager for some of the players on the Bengals. For years I observed his admirable work ethics up close. And I can assure you that the same fierce determination, hard work, and personal endurance that drove Louis to all of his accomplishments and success in pro football are the same characteristics that make him and his company a highly recommended partner to work with. And it won't take you long to become friends because of the personal attention Louis gives all his customers. Give him a call, you'll see what I mean. You can reach Louis at 513-489-6600 or fax him at 513-605-3050. Be sure to tell him I said hello and mention that I referred you.

### Motivational do's and don't's

**1** **DON'T** *ship the gift to your employee's address.*
**DO** *have the gifts delivered to your company in your name.*

This creates double stimulation. First, when the gift arrives, take the opportunity to recognize the employee in front of their co-workers by congratulating them when you present the gift. An employee is highly stimulated when he receives what he earned in front of his peers and is recognized by management. And as a result, everyone else becomes eager for his or her turn. Second, the employee now takes his gift home where he will again be in the spotlight for his achievement.

**2** **DON'T** *tax your people on their gifts.*
**DO** *create a system through your accountant or controller that does not tax your employees on the prizes they earn.*

I've seen this both ways and believe me, there is a major difference in the employee perception of this program. Picture this: one of your employees works hard and earns enough points for a television, orders it, it comes in, you present it with congratulations and then you say, "By the way, you might want to set aside about $35 to cover the tax on this. OUCH! Talk about counterproductive! Work out a 'gross-up' situation with your

5

accountant so the taxes are absorbed into the bonus structure without impacting the employee.

**3** **DON'T** *use points for only commission or bonus.*
**DO** *use points for contest prizes, perfect attendance and, on spontaneous occasions, in addition to commission and bonus.*

Another great benefit of this program is the chance to stimulate people at any time by rewarding them with 'point checks' at times other than the expected commission or bonus. I know what you're thinking, "Where do I get the extra points?" There are two ways. First, when you structure your commission/bonus plan, leave room for additional points above and beyond the total figure. Second, and probably more practical, be creative with some of the unearned points. Think about it. Not every employee will hit maximum commission or bonus levels every month or quarter. As those 'unearned' points grow, you can draw from that pool and utilize points in many valuable ways. And most important, you're not increasing your budget to do it. Remember that your budget has already been established and you're in control of the point checks. This is a little different than a cash system, isn't it? Unless you feel you can you get your company to promptly cut you an additional check on the spot whenever you need or want one? Yeah...right!

Contest prizes are a great way to put some of those unearned points to 'motivational use.' My belief in the power of contests is no secret in our industry. Establish creative contests with various point totals for prizes. You will gain improved productivity and enthusiasm without spending outside your budget. It's a win/win for everyone.

Also, draw from your point 'pool' for individual or team performance-related achievements, consistent attendance or other spontaneous reasons. I'm not suggesting you use up all the budgeted points just because you have them. But it sure works out well to have that resource to draw from whenever needed.

## A Final Thought

The success of a catalog/point system in our industry is not theoretical. I'm not hoping this will work for you. It will work!

If you are currently using this system and it is working well, I applaud you. If it was unsuccessful, dig into it and uncover the problems. There isn't any reason for this system not to be enormously successful. Or if you are looking for new ways to create and maintain an enthusiastic, productive environment, **this is it.** I challenge you to climb out of the old paradigm, "Cash is the way we've always done it." Give your people the opportunity to purchase enjoyable things they would never normally have the cash to buy.

This idea doesn't cost you any more money, it couldn't be easier to implement, your employees will love it and I've done the work of finding you a good company. So . . . are you going to let the fire in your employees' pockets continue to burn? Because as it burns out, so will your people.

# 2

# Recognition and Attention

If I had arranged this book in order of importance, this chapter would still be right up near the top. How often do you recognize your employees for their achievements? I think if we all had to address that question, the answer in most cases would be "not enough, not nearly enough." When your employees accomplish something, your recognition is their appreciation. Close your eyes and think back to the last time that you received recognition from your boss. When was the last time he or she said "Great job" or passed you a note describing his appreciation for you and the job you do? For most of you, I'd be inclined to believe you'd have to say it's been a long time. It's sad but true. I firmly believe that most telemarketing managers don't give enough recognition because they don't get enough. And if you don't receive it, it doesn't come naturally to give it out. If this applies to you, I propose you drop this excuse like a bad habit.

I could retire if I had a dollar for every time my mother said, "If Johnny jumps off the bridge does that mean you have to jump off the bridge too?" But now I know she was right. Even if you don't get enough recognition, this is not a reason not to give it to your people.

Consider the price of recognition and attention; dollar-wise, it's free. The only cost to you is time. And while time is in short supply in your busy schedule, recognition doesn't take long. It shows your employees that you care and, as my father often reminded me, "People don't care how much you know until they know how much you care."

Verbal recognition is so easy to give and it means so much to the person receiving it. There isn't a day that goes by that I don't tell someone who deserves it, "Thanks for a great day," or "I appreciate your efforts, thanks." A simple thank-you for a productive day or a job accomplished means a great deal to most people. There isn't a corner drug dealer in the world that can supply people with a better or more effective upper than this. (I often worry that the mob is going to send Rocco and Vito to pay me a visit for hurting the business!) And when you give this verbal recognition, do it in front of other employees whenever possible. Do you know what effect this has? Think of how it would make you feel. It makes you feel even better so it's that much more effective when other employees are within hearing range. These "public strokes" become the instant envy of others and encourages them to earn some of this recognition and attention. I don't know about you, but I have often had the luxury of beginning the workday with some general announcements. While these announcements generally include policy changes and selling tips, this time offers the perfect stage for handing out some verbal academy awards.

On these days I recognize people for notable individual performances, positive attitude or sometimes an achievement in their personal lives. Often I will have come up to the front so I can shake their hand or high-five them in front of everyone. People naturally want what other people are getting especially when it comes to attention. If you have kids, I'm sure you can relate to what happens in my house. My daughter Jackie is in high school and sometimes our moments together are rare. We may be sitting on the couch together in front of the TV or relaxing and talking about our days and then our quality time comes to a halt. My 12-year-old Danny, who is the largest beneficiary of time with Dad, will try to nuzzle his way in between Jackie and me. Why? For the attention. Danny wants what Jackie is getting, and Jackie accepts the challenge by cuddling up a little closer to me, just to make her point. And with Michelle in college and working these days, we seldom have all five of us eating dinner together as a family. This has always been important to us so when we do, each child gets a chance to talk about his or her day. It's fun to watch as one of them will talk about something that prompts acknowledgement from Kathy and I—and boom! One of the others will be quick to tell of something similar in search of the same attention. And why not? It's normal and natural and it's no different with your employees. They love it when you give them attention. And that love grows tenfold when that attention comes in front of their peers.

If your company has voice mail, this is a great resource for verbally recognizing people. Leave recognition messages for employees and send a copy of the same message to your boss. This gives added motivational value to the message. Think about it, an employee goes into his voice mail box for the usual messages and unexpectedly gets to listen to a message of recognition from his supervisor or manager. That will be enough to offset the stress accumulated by the usual messages that relate to extra work, project deadlines, and meetings.

**MEETINGS** are a good place to verbally recognize your employees. I know what you're thinking, "No, please don't even mention the M-word. My life is meetings, I go to meetings to decide what we should talk about in the next meeting." I understand. I know this word should only be whispered and that to some of you it's almost a swear word. We'd all like to avoid meetings as much as we used to avoid the evil green vegetable on our dinner plates when we were kids (mine was asparagus). But on the upside, meetings offer a perfect chance to motivate your employees whether they attend the meeting or not. Let's look at both possibilities.

Picture yourself in a meeting that includes one or more of your employees and your boss. You need to find a spot where you can recognize the achievements of one or more of the employees present at the meeting. This could happen when the subject matter becomes a segue for verbal recognition or you can simply lead off the meeting by announcing that you'd like to share some exciting news before the meeting gets underway. And then you can brag about the achievements you wish to recognize. Talk about making your employees feel great. There they are, in front of other company employees including your boss, while you are boasting about them. And while they may appear to be feeling shy and or even undeserving, don't let them fool you. They are loving every bit of it. And if you have more than one employee in there, you're creating double stimulation again. This creates motivation for the employee you're recognizing while also motivating your other employees who are present since they will want the public attention their colleague is receiving. We talked about this human envy earlier in the chapter. It's only natural and it works every time.

What about if the employee you're recognizing is not present at the meeting? This is also effective. Think about it. You brag about an employee's accomplishments during a meeting. Later that day, someone that was in the meeting sees that special employee and he will congratulate him and tell him about the attention you gave him. This will probably happen several times as different people from the same meeting acknowledge that employee. It's inevitable and it's effective. And imagine if some of your other employees were in the meeting but not the one you recognized. That will only increase the effectiveness. They will surely get the word back to the rest of your division quickly, as well as to your target employee.

Recognizing employees at meetings generates some powerful motivational mileage. And maybe you can look at meetings differently from now on. If you must attend them, use them as an easy opportunity for employee motivation.

**SOCIAL GATHERINGS** and special occasions are also fine opportunities for verbal recognition. Christmas parties, summer picnics and contest trips are just a few examples of company-sponsored events where you can score big motivational points with your employees. We've talked about the power of motivating people in general and how this increases when it's done in front of their peers and how it increases further when it's in front of company executives. Well, just when you thought there was no way to make the impact any bigger . . . bring on the family.

Any time you can recognize an employee in front of his spouse, children, or family, jump on it. It's naturally stimulating for a person to receive praise in front of family members. Again, put yourself in those shoes. I can't imagine that your entire life has passed without getting some type of recognition in front of your family. Remember open house at school when you were a kid? I guess if you're my age it's probably a little fuzzy. But I can still remember how good it made me feel when my teachers would commend me to my parents. Remember that indescribable feeling of pride? Or guys, remember little league baseball? Remember your coach getting the team huddled together after a great game with all the parents listening anxiously nearby, and he compliments you for a key hit or a great catch? Wasn't that feeling unbelievable? Recently, I have also been the parent watching as my son anxiously looks over to make sure Kath and I heard every word of praise as his coach says, "Danny, you pitched a great game today!" You've heard that some kids never grow up? When it comes to recognition in front of family members, maybe we're all kids and we never grow up. Is it any different with your employees? Of course it isn't. Let's look at a few family opportunities for gaining some serious motivational mileage.

Do you have a department or company Christmas party each year? If not, you should. Getting together at this time of year is valuable as it helps in setting a positive tone for the upcoming year. It doesn't have to be a lavish layout, nor does it have to involve some great expense. What's important is that couples or families get together outside of the workplace at this time of year that's associated with sharing. If this is an annual event for you I encourage you to continue it. If not, let's get the Grinch out of your system and enjoy the season.

**Christmas parties** certainly provide a perfect setting for handing out some early gifts in the form of verbal recognition. During the blessing of the food, be sure to give thanks for your employees and their families. If you have a gift exchange, you should play Santa by handing out the gifts and saying something complimentary to each person. I have also spontaneously toasted exceptional accomplishments during a special occasion like this.

**Summer picnics** are motivational within themselves and present the same recognition opportunities that Christmas parties offer. Get the idea? Any time you're in the presence of your employees' families, you're sitting on a golden opportunity to give deserving people special attention that will pay big dividends.

Using these two examples of social gatherings, let your mind wonder and see how many other special occasions you can come up with that will also provide the stage for handing out these verbal Oscars to your people. Also, consider the countless opportunities you've missed in the past. If you're like most people, the number is staggering. But that's the past, right? Create some opportunities for families to spend time together and when you do, tell the families how proud you are of your employee's achievements.

While verbal recognition is extremely effective, **written recognition** is equally stimulating and visibly lasts longer. This being the case, I always wonder why people don't send acknowledgements more often. When was the last time you received a letter from your boss recognizing any of your accomplishments? In the past week? Month? Year? Ever? If you have received one, how did it make you feel? Terrific, right? Let's take a closer look at the power of written recognition and consider when and how to use it.

Short letters or memos expressing your appreciation will create instant stimulation and long-lasting motivation. First we'll consider the letter.

Imagine getting home from work one day and finding a letter in the mail from your boss recognizing you for a special achievement at work. First you feel an immediate rush of excitement. And then follows the long-lasting motivator, the letter is yours to have and to hold forever. Two strokes of stimulation for the price of one [postage stamp]. Although the first wave of pride will fade, it will be renewed every time the employee looks at your letter. And believe me, they will read it again and again. Most people make a point of keeping it in a highly visible place. Routinely, this treasured piece will wind up back at work after the family has seen it. And usually it gets hung in the employee's workstation for everyone else to admire, and becomes what I refer to as hanging stimulation.

You can use motivational letters for a variety of situations such as after a productive week, month, or year, or spontaneously for different achievements. There are other ways I have also found successful. Whenever you get ready to announce a big sales contest, make sure you send a letter to your employees' homes explaining the contest, laying out the guidelines and goals for winning and most important, describing the prizes. Do you understand the power in this letter? Not only is the family aware of what they could win, they also know what dad or mom must accomplish to win the contest. You have now turned everyday suburban families into cheerleading, motivational allies. Their kids' daily questions and interest have now graduated from "How was your day?" to "Hey, Mom (or Dad), did you hit your goal today?" or "Are you still on track to win the contest?" And even if there are no kids, the old spouse pressure will suffice. Spouses will naturally be excited about whatever contest your employee has a chance to win and therefore join in the "encouragement" of the employee's effort. Now let's explore the concept of encouragement. While Webster defines encourage as give support to, be favorable to, foster help, he forgot some key elements like the specific definition for spouse encouragement in a situation like this. Of course there will be the usual good old-fashioned support here. But in terms of fostering help, here's where the definition gets stretched just a bit. Fostering help can now be properly defined as encouragement through pressure. What used to be "Have a good day, Honey," becomes "Honey, you better have a good day, don't forget what we're working for." The bottom line is that informing the family brings family support, and family support can only help everyone. And make sure you take advantage of the obvious opportunity that follows the contest. I'm referring to the motivation you create when you send the contest winner a letter of congratulations. Make sure you put it on company letterhead and address the envelope to "The Family of [employee's name]." As the saying goes, this will put the icing on the cake. As an example, the following letter is one that I wrote to employees in the spring of 1997 congratulating the winners of a weekend getaway contest.

June 14, 1997

Joe Winner & Family
12345 Main Street
Buhl, AL 35446

Dear Joe and Family,

Just a quick note to congratulate you on the tremendous effort you displayed in winning one of the hotel rooms for our 2nd annual Gulf Shores trip! It was a long contest and only 11 out of 56 employees were able to achieve the necessary qualifications to win. You've heard the expression "hard work pays off"? It sure does.

Thank you again Joe for your outstanding accomplishment. With employees like you it is easy to understand why our company continues to grow and prosper. Grab your sunglasses, swimsuits, and suntan lotion. I look forward to seeing you, Jane and the boys.

Dave

Short, simple, and very effective. During our weekend together, every family mentioned their letter at least once. I hope these ideas will get your juices flowing and your mind working overtime to think of different ways and occasions where letters can be used as effective non-monetary motivation.

Earlier I mentioned **memos** as a form of written recognition. These will also become hanging stimulation because most employees will display them in their work areas after showing them to family, friends and—most important—their co-workers. "What's the big deal?" you ask. It's not a big deal, unless you make it one. How? Number one, make sure you copy his or her immediate supervisor (if there is one) and executive management. The stimulation from a memo recognizing outstanding achievement gets an upgrade when the employee knows his supervisors and or managers have received a copy. Number two, be expressive, not mundane. Your efforts and intentions are wasted if the content of your memo is dry and lacking in any apparent excitement.

Let me show you what I mean. Look at the following memo that someone sent to an employee:

> "Thank you for doing a great job on your 4th quarter project. It really helped our year-end on a positive note. We appreciate your effort."

Effective? I guess it could be. Boring? Definitely. Let's see how we can say the same thing with a little more enthusiasm:

> "Congratulations [Name]!! Your outstanding effort has helped put us over the top for the 4th quarter. My grade on your project on a scale from 1–10 is an 11! Employee dedication like yours is why our company continues to grow and prosper."

The content is the same but now the message has some new energy. The more expressive you are the bigger the impression your message will make. Don't be afraid to be creative. Number

3, my version of the K.I.S.S. theory is **Keep It Short and Simple.** There is no need for this type of memo to be long and drawn out, unless of course you want to diminish its value. Think about the last time you were in the audience at a seminar listening to a presentation. Remember the speakers who made one or two good points and then put you to sleep by dragging on and on? Don't let yourself get lost in the false theory that more words create a higher impact. Too many words will have a lesser value. Keep it short and to the point, copy immediate supervisors and executive management whenever possible, pack it with enthusiasm and then step back, grab a Coke and watch the positive results.

A few more ideas for utilizing this powerful form of non-monetary motivation include company newsletters, a special corkboard for departmental news and information, visible achievement boards and daily goal or quota cards. I have successfully used all four of these venues for written recognition.

Does your organization have an **in-house newsletter** that reaches all employees with the news and views about your company? This is yet another perfect showcase to put your employee's name in lights when he deserves it. Most newsletters have a special place for employee recognition and or breaking news about a department. Whenever possible, include a picture of the person along with the story. And remember that the anticipation of the newsletter release is as stimulating as the article itself, if you'll do what it takes to make this waiting time exciting.

> **DON'T** *just submit the information and forget about it until the newsletter is delivered.*
> **DO** *keep a copy of your information and you can easily create stimulation through anticipation.*

During the waiting time, periodically hang up a teaser in a visible spot in your department. My teasers usually consist of a large bold title such as COMING SOON or ON ITS WAY on bright paper, with further reminders below that sometimes include quotes from your copy of the story.

I know what you're thinking. "Does this really make a difference?" Think about the special events in your life such as birthdays, vacations and holiday times. Close your eyes and go back to your childhood. Remember the feelings of anxiety you had before your birthday? About the presents you might get and how special the day would be? Weren't the few weeks before just as stimulating as the actual day itself? And holiday times? What about the weeks before Christmas? And what about looking forward to that glorious extended break from school? As the days were counted down, the excitement mounted. And what about your more recent vacations? Wouldn't you agree that the time and energy you spend preparing and thinking about a vacation is almost as exciting as the vacation itself?

Did you ever order anything with cereal box tops? Remember that one painful sentence in small print that we all hated? "Please allow 4-6 weeks for delivery." AAHHHH! Four to six weeks? You must be kidding, that's a lifetime. My mom was skilled at building anticipation, giving me constant reminders of what was ahead. We would cross out each day on a calendar or she would remind me every few days that the big date was coming. When the box finally arrived from General Mills I was practically foaming at the mouth. As I look back, the anticipation prior to the actual delivery was probably more exciting than the silly little thing that arrived in the box. Anyway it was hardly ever as good as it looked on the back of the box, right?

As far as I can tell, maybe as adults we're really not that different than kids. And neither are your employees. The point is simple. If you periodically remind your employees in creative ways of the upcoming issue of the newsletter [in which they are appearing], you maximize the anticipation and this ultimately increases the motivation.

19

| WEEKLY LEADERS | | | | | | | |
|---|---|---|---|---|---|---|---|
| Name | # of Calls | Name | # Presentations | Name | Sale $'s | Name | 1st orders |
| Arlene T | 324 | Melissa W | 65 | Sharon | 32,846.44 | Roger | 12 |
| Karey | 294 | Marcia | 59 | Kristi | 31,235.4 | Jolene | 12 |
| John | 279 | Jolene | 55 | Paula | 29,185.23 | Rene | 10 |
| Roger | 277 | Arlene T | 53 | Julie | 27,549.99 | John | 10 |
| Linda | 271 | Linda | 52 | Carl | 25,519.96 | Becky | 10 |
| Leslie | 267 | Becky | 50 | Rick | 25,303.09 | Karey | 10 |
| Carl | 266 | Roger | 49 | Dean | 25,120.38 | Brenda | 10 |
| Jolene | 262 | Stan | 47 | Karey | 25,052.46 | Michelle | 9 |
| Heather | 259 | Karen | 47 | Leslie | 22,895.23 | Paula | 9 |
| Keith | 256 | Jeff | 46 | Wendy | 22,144.98 | Amy F | 9 |
| Stan | 254 | Jacki | 43 | Jolene | 20,889.99 | David | 9 |
| Kathy N | 253 | Angie P | 41 | Amy F | 20,367.81 | Heather | 9 |
| Rene | 252 | Deb | 40 | David | 20,049.37 | Bridget | 9 |
| Rick | 252 | Lavonda | 34 | Janice | 20,304.15 | Leslie | 8 |
| Brenda | 251 | Kim | 34 | Angela | 19,496.71 | Joyce/Porter | 8 |

**Dave's achievement board**

Have you ever put up **achievement boards** in your department to show your employees' performance on a weekly or monthly basis? If not, you should be doing this. The boards are easy to prepare and they continue to pay motivational dividends week after week, month after month. Why? You've displayed your employees' performance numbers for everyone to see, good or bad. First I hang a large banner that says Wall of Fame. We're already off to a motivational start. The word 'fame' makes your employees want to be up there because you've designated this as a special place, a place where others will associate your name with achievements above the norm. Then purchase some large dry erase boards (mine are 4'x 8'), enough to fit all of your employees names (each board fits about 40 names) and striping tape in different colors from your office supply house. Hang these boards in your department in a visible location. Decide on how many categories you want to highlight. Then tape an appropriate matrix on each board accordingly to fit the names and numbers you want to include each week. A picture of one of my current boards is pictured above

I currently track four categories in our sales division (sales volume, number of new accounts, number of presentations, number of phone calls) on a weekly basis that I highlight on our boards. I call the program The Sales Achievement Club. Each week everyone's performance is listed in chronological order from the best to the worst in each category. I highlight the top performer in red. The second through fifth places are in blue and everyone else is in black. People gain Club status each month by being one of the top five (three points for each first place finish, two points for second place and one point for third). I hold a special lunch every month for these five top people and I include incentives like prize drawings. But the real value of this program is the motivation generated by the weekly boards. There it is in plain sight, each person's performance, great, good, mediocre, bad or horrible. It's up there and they know its going to be up there. For some people the scores give recognition and for some it means embarrassment, but overall the system offers stimulation. If an employee's numbers are good they naturally want to stay at the top. If their numbers are low, they're not going to want to stay at the bottom for long. Most of all, these boards are positive recognition for those achieving the highest success

Another easy idea for written recognition is **weekly goal cards.** The one I developed and use for my outbound survey department is pictured on the next page. Weekly goal cards are easy to create and extremely effective. My employees fill out their weekly goals and then sign next to the line "I WILL HIT MY GOAL." Then they hang it up front and center in their work area (where they look at it every day, all week long). I know what you're thinking now. "Why is this considered written recognition?" It's not yet, but it will be next week. Every week, those who reach 100% of their goals get to pin their goal cards up on

# GOAL CARD

Name: _____ Supv: _____ Week Ending _____

## I will hit my goals this week:

### Goals: Calls _____ New Accounts _____

| | Calls | | | New Accts | |
|---|---|---|---|---|---|
| | Goal | | +/- | Goal | +/- |
| Monday | | | | | |
| Tuesday | | | | | |
| Wednesday | | | | | |
| Thursday | | | | | |
| Friday | | | | | |
| TOTALS | | | | | |

## I did hit my goals this week!!

**GOALS:** "The magic begins when you set goals…it is then that the switch is turned on, the current begins to flow and the power to accomplish becomes a reality a special corkboard on our Wall of Fame titled GOAL BUSTERS! (pictured below). So all week those goal cards remain on the special board for everyone to gawk at and then the process begins all over again. Each week, the board is cleared off preparing it for next week's pin-ups.

What about the 100% goal cards that we pull off the board each week? Do you think we throw them away? Not on your life. I return them to the employees, with two important additions. First, I put a positive sticker in the top right corner that says "Great Job," "Nice Work," "You Did It," etc. (You can purchase these stickers at card shops or teaching supply stores.) Then I take a blue, red or green Sharpie and write a message of congratulations or appreciation and sign it. Then it goes back to the employee. Does it sound like a lot of work? It really isn't, but even if it were I'd still do it. It's worth it. A simple message like "Strong effort, thanks" or "Hard work pays off, thanks,"

**Dave's "Goal Busters" board**

handwritten and signed by you will pay back ten times over. Like the letters and memos, these become long-term motivators because people decorate their areas with them for everyone to see. Egomaniacs, you say? I don't think so. They're human beings like you and me. They are proud of their accomplishments and want to show off the recognition they receive. This is absolutely 100% normal behavior. So why not capitalize on it? While many employees display their goal cards in different ways, some of my best employees wallpaper their workstations with them. Once again, you, the leader, gain double stimulation here. Number one, these cards stimulate the person who earned them, got them back, and looks at them everyday. Number two, they entice the other employees, who also want as many as possible. You can draw these goal cards on a computer (two cards per page) and copy and cut them at the local printer. You have no excuse not to use this easy, inexpensive resource that will foster more motivation for your employees.

**A Sales News board** visibly placed in your department is another means for spreading the recognition. Mine is a simple corkboard (3' x 4') titled Sales News and Info. You can display pictures of company events as well as positive customer letters you receive. (The originals should have a brief note from you, copied to your boss, and then go to the appropriate employee.) This also includes copies of recognition memos or letters written to employees and any personal employee publicity that takes place outside of the workplace (newspaper stories, church bulletin, school system newsletter, etc.).

This highly visible Sales News board will help your people learn more about each other while producing employee motivation by recognizing employees' personal achievements as well as professional accomplishments. There must be countless other ideas you can run with. These are my favorites that have brought me a great deal of success in my environments. The old theory that "no news is good news" is just that, old and outdated. Throw it out with yesterday's paper.

Along with the power of verbal and written recognition comes what I'd have to call physical recognition, the good old-fashioned round of applause. Why this simple and effective form of recognition is rarely used is beyond me. Well, tell me, when was the last time your colleagues gave you a round of applause? When was the last time you initiated a round of applause for one of your employees? If you are one of the few who can say you've done this recently, congratulations. But if you're like most people who would have to answer with something like, "I can't remember," or "a couple of years ago," or worse, "never," then listen up. Here comes what is affectionately known as a quick fix.

**A round of applause** is without question one of the easiest motivators you could invest your energy in. First, let's explore the power of applause. Think of how you felt when you received applause for something. You probably feel awkward and humbled like most of us and pretend you don't deserve it ("Ah, it's no big deal...don't do that.") While you were putting on a show of humility on the outside, I know exactly what was happening on the inside and so do you! You were celebrating the applause and enjoying the attention. And maybe silently you wanted them to stand up and continue. Come on, admit it so we can move on. It feels awesome right? Of course it does. While it may be a little embarrassing at times it doesn't even come close to the emotional high that people experience when the applause is for them. It's a rush. Imagine as I often do what the final day leader at the Masters golf tournament feels like as he walks up the famous 18th fairway toward the green to the thunderous ovation that only Augusta National could provide. Or how it must feel for the U.S. Women's Open Tennis Champion to stand at center court as she holds up the trophy to the deafening applause that fills the stadium. Is the hair on your back standing up? Are there chills down your spine?

While our jobs may not be related to professional golf or tennis, the need for appreciation is no different. To make a significant contribution, to complete a special project, to set a new sales or performance record is your employee's trophy, his moment. And you can make that moment even more special by recognizing it with applause. Above all, it's easy to find situations to use applause as a motivational tool. Earlier we mentioned **meetings** as a perfect opportunity to verbally recognize someone. It is also the chance to recognize someone with applause. I sometimes schedule meetings for that sole purpose, just to recognize the outstanding achievements of one person or a group of employees. Why not? We all know the usual feelings you have as you head for meetings, counting up all the things you should be doing instead, and then—bang! Someone is getting major recognition in front of the others with a round of applause. It's surprising at times and effective every time.

We also talked about social gatherings being a great opportunity to verbally recognize employees in front of friends and family with some words of thanks for their accomplishments. Well, here is one more ingredient for the mix. When you acknowledge them for their achievements or contributions, add the round of applause. Talk about total stimulation! While the person is there amongst his family and his colleagues' families, you are stimulating him and everyone else because they're going to want this too. Now they will go back and work harder to get it. Without question, this is a win/win/win situation. Did you catch that? Win, win, win. Where did the third win come from? We just established that. The first win is the stimulation that happens to the applause recipient and the second win is the stimulation that motivates the others that witnessed the applause. The third win? That's you. You're the overall winner here, you and certainly your company. The motivation created by the applause will inspire higher levels of performance from your people so they can get more and more applause. It's a beautiful productive cycle and it will just continue in that direction if you keep the applause happening in your environment. And it doesn't cost you a penny. Now let's add up the return on your investment: happier, more dedicated employees with higher levels of performance who stay on the job longer. In one word, immeasurable.

Let me share one major caution regarding all forms of employee recognition. **Only those who achieve should receive recognition.** Be careful not to overuse or equally recognize the underachievers. If you do—and believe me, I've made this mistake, the message associated with your recognition will be seriously diminished because it is no longer special.

Otherwise, recognize your people and do it often and in different ways both verbally, in writing, and with applause. Remember that the cost is free, except for time. But as discussed earlier, time means you care. Ask yourself, "How much do I care?" Only you can answer that. But remember, if you don't care, neither will your employees.

# 3

# Time Off

In the telemarketing industry where burnout and turnover are waiting to happen, time off is the biggest motivator. Maybe some of you just turned white with panic or red with rage and you're thinking, "Is this guy nuts?" Just like you, I need my people to stay on the phone all the time. During some recent consulting projects, company executives contested that their sales people were paid to be on the phone so why should we give them time off? I was able to educate them in how to utilize time off as an advantage to the employee and the company. And I explained that I am not referring to huge chunks of time away from the office.

If you're like the rest of us, you're always trying to maximize the performance of your people without giving away an extra penny, right? The good news is that you don't need to spend the extra penny. Giving them time off is actually more effective and it doesn't cost you a cent. The key lies in setting appropriate goals and productivity objectives. If you set the performance level above what you would normally get from the employee, this incentive is a win/win.

Let's take a minute to make sure you're digesting this concept. This is too important to rush through. Time off is a prime incentive and a treasured prize. Your job is to structure the goal so that your employee's performance exceeds the norm. This means that when someone reaches the goal and earns time off, he has already exceeded your expectations. If he wins time off, you win, the company wins and the employee wins. Everyone comes out ahead. Now we'll consider the increments of time off, how you can track the time earned, and most importantly, successful ways to use this incentive.

First, there is really no magic to the time increments you decide to use. I use a wide variety, from fifteen-minute segments to full days off. As I said before, as long as the productivity goal you put in place outweighs the time off you give, everyone comes out ahead.

To keep track of the time earned, you can use several methods. One way that has always worked well for me is using my business cards with a special stamp on the back that says "15 minutes," "30 minutes," etc. I sign them for validation and hand them out accordingly. Whatever method you use, don't make the mistake that I made. The first time I tried keeping track I used Monopoly money for increments of minutes. Pretty smart, right? Right. A twenty-dollar bill meant twenty minutes off, and so on. Very dumb, right? Also right. It wasn't too long before people were gathering a lot more Monopoly bills than I thought I'd given out. They quickly figured out they could grab a few bills from their Monopoly games at home and bring them to work! Well, after recovering from temporary brain damage, I realized I better validate the time off in more controlled ways. I continue using Monopoly money but I also validate the bills with special stamps and my signature.

I also use other methods of tracking time off. I use gigantic plastic quarters to represent one quarter of an hour. These are sold at party supplies stores. The log system is another method. This bookkeeping does not have to be complicated and is actually little more than a list of your employees. Whenever someone earns time off, you log it by his (her) name. Whenever someone uses his time off you subtract it so you can always see the balance.

I also use handwritten messages reading, "Congratulations, you just won 1 hour off!" Then I sign it and deliver it to them in an envelope. While computer-written messages may be neater, handwritten messages always mean more to the employee. If you've ever received a homemade card from your kids, you know what I mean. When my children make me a card by hand for my birthday or Father's Day, the homemade card means so much more than any store bought card. These messages are no different.

I have also used a log system to ensure that everyone's time off is documented when they earn it and then properly subtracted as they use it. This can be a simple list of employees. Whenever anyone earns time off it is logged by the employee's name. Whenever they use it, it is subtracted so we both know how much is left for use.

Now let's look at some specific ways you can use this inspirational tool and enjoy the resulting boost in performance, productivity and positive morale.

### Go-Home Goals

Just as time off has proven to be a better motivator than even cash, 'go-home' goals have proven to be one of the best ways to utilize time off. Set up performance goals that represent 110 to120 percent of your employees' normal daily production. Then let them leave two or three hours early any day they reach the goal. That's right, two or three hours early. There's no typo here. You'll be impressed by how your employees will rise to this occasion. It's unbelievable how hard people will push when they know they can leave two to three hours early by exceeding the daily expectation by only 10 to 20 percent.

As an example, following is a program I have used for my sales people: 120 percent of their daily goal allows them to leave at 2:30 instead of 5:00 on any day they reach it, as long as they are caught up for the week (we use a weekly quota system). In other words, an employee must have met 100 percent of his or her weekly goal to qualify. For instance, if 'Joe' had a slow Monday or Tuesday but hits 100 percent of his daily goal on Wednesday, he's still only at 92 percent of his three-day goal so he does not qualify to leave early on Wednesday. This type of program also ensures that each week people get off to a strong start so that they can take advantage of this perk as many days as possible. Does this inspire them to perform? How about a "9. 7" on the Richter scale! I've had people make plans days in advance to ensure that they force themselves to work hard. This drives them to do whatever it takes to enjoy nine holes of golf, shopping at the mall, picking up the kids from school or any other activities we all wish we were doing at that time of day.

This system also works well in the business-to-consumer world that involves night shifts. Who wouldn't want to leave work early on any shift? Probably nobody. I have also used weekly go-home goals that follow the same format. Just figure out a percentage above their weekly goal that represents more than the time you will be letting them off and you're on your way. If an employee hits 130 percent of his (her) weekly goal he can leave at lunch on Friday. By reaching 150 percent of his weekly goal he earns the whole day off. That's right, all day Friday. Now before you have a coronary attack, just relax for a minute and consider the stakes. If you receive 150 percent of someone's expected performance, why should you mind if they're gone all day Friday? If the go-home goal were not in place, you probably wouldn't have received the additional percentage over their goal, right? And let's face it, when someone hits the 100 percent mark, what happens? They stop, of course. Then they find something else to do, something other than being on the telephone. And those other things include distracting other employees who haven't reached their goals yet. And sometimes they may engage in an activity that's affectionately known as 'sale bagging,' making the sales but holding them for another time

31

when they need them. WARNING: This is a game that hurts everybody. Holding a sale means that the customers wind up being misled about delivery times. Also, sales people tend to use this trick as a crutch and it becomes a bad habit. The good news is that with weekly go-home goals in place, this will never happen. Employees will use every sale to reach their quotas and take advantage of a long weekend. That's what I would do. Wouldn't you?

Although leaving work early may not inspire everyone, it will always motivate the majority of the people. I've seen the productivity and revenue rise. And I've heard the same positive reports from many companies after I've helped them implement these daily and weekly go-home goals. It works.

You can also use this tool on a spontaneous basis. After a slow week, you can come in Friday morning and announce a team productivity goal for the day. Once the team meets the goal, they can all go home for the weekend. The gain for you is obvious. If the week has been less than productive, the odds are that no one would reach their quotas even with a good day Friday. But once you announce the Friday plan, the sudden opportunity inspires them to drive harder. They'll finish up the week with a good day for the reward of a short workday. In this case, you draw a stronger performance out of this group than you would have without the go-home incentive. This strategy inspires people whether they have reached their weekly goals or not. And in both cases, you win. Those who were behind for the week now have one more reason to push. Those who have already achieved their goals already used up their motivation, but now you've re-inspired them to keep on pushing so they can leave early.

Let me add one caution. Do not overuse this Friday strategy. Reserve it as a surprise for rare occasions, very rare occasions. Otherwise you'll be shooting yourself in the foot like I've done more than once. If people anticipate a Friday goal day, they have less incentive to push hard early in the week. Make sure you keep this one in the closet like the good set of dishes that are not for routine use. Go-home goals will bring you big results when you use them properly. And while this incentive may reward your employees with many hours of time off, do not underestimate the value of getting even just a few extra minutes of precious time off. Here's a few ways to effectively use smaller portions of time off that will motivate your people.

### Extended/Additional Breaks

If you're asking, "Breaks? What breaks?" please consider my next recommendation. In this profession, breaks are needed, and in most cases, much deserved. Your employees need some scheduled ten- to fifteen-minute breaks. Think about it. What do people usually do during a break? They go outside for a quick cigarette or they get a snack from the vending machine because that's all that short time will allow. Now, what would it mean to have an extra fifteen minutes of break time—an extended break? Well, suddenly you have time to run to the bank, head home for a minute if you live nearby, go out for an ice cream, do some homework, or run an errand that you couldn't even think about during a normal fifteen-minute break. In other words, a little extension on a break can make a big difference. In fact, you can offer these fifteen-minute time-off rewards in the form of additional breaks. Some people would rather have another short break later than a longer extended break. Both of these options work well, especially if you give your employees a choice.

### Extended Lunch

This idea is geared for the business-to-business arena with full-time employees who usually work 8:00 to 5:00, with lunch squeezed in somewhere. (In the business-to- consumer industry, the shifts typically run part-time four to five hours, so this opportunity does not usually apply here.) The plastic quarters work well here, as do the other time-off prizes (including one half-hour or even one hour). If a thirty- to sixty-minute lunch sounds familiar, you know that many of your employees wish it were longer. For the same reasons that extended breaks can be useful to your employees, extended lunches are equally attractive. This allows time for lunch plus errands, maybe a visit home, a long lunch visit with friends or colleagues, etc. No matter how you slice it, extra time away from the office is always an incentive.

## Late Arrival / Early Dismissal

Time off can also be offered in any environment as a late arrival to work. In fact, this has always been a favorite use of time off. The luxury of delaying your arrival by even fifteen or thirty minutes means a great deal to most people, especially in our industry. Think about it. When you're in the habit of getting up at a certain time to get ready for work, even a few minutes of grace is reason for celebration. We've all done it. We set the alarm a little bit later and when it goes off maybe we hit the snooze and roll over to the cool side of the pillow for just a little longer. Isn't that the greatest feeling? The same holds true for afternoon and evening shifts. Instead of catching a few more 'ZZZs' before coming in, the earned late arrival allows the employee to possibly have dinner with the family, get some homework done or run a couple of errands before arriving at work. It offers the same kind of value that most employees warmly welcome. And they will appreciate the chance to earn it.

The same incentive holds true for an early dismissal. If cornered for the most popular use of time off, I would say this is it. We've already discussed the incentive of daily and weekly go-home goals. In addition, you can command some serious motivation with small amounts of strategic time off. Holidays are a perfect opportunity for a spontaneous gesture on your part as managers. Jump into your time capsule and go back to the past holidays and most importantly, to the day of work prior to that holiday vacation. About one half-hour before the end of the shift, what happens? Holiday excitement takes over and very little work gets done, that's what happens. Sometimes I will let everyone go thirty minutes early on that day. I have also used this spontaneous gesture on other rare occasions for reasons I call just because. Just because our division set a new sales record, just because it was beautiful outside or just because I wanted to. The motivational payback will far outweigh the production you 'lost' in the last thirty minutes of that day, anytime and every time. There is always something special about being able to leave work early.

Also, since we're talking about non-monetary motivation, time off makes a worthy prize for contests. You don't need to be handing cash to the winners all the time when you can offer them time off. In fact, given the choice of prizes, many will select time off rather than cash. And whenever you use time off as a contest prize, be sure to add one stipulation. Employees can only use the time off when they are 100 percent caught up for the week. Again, use your log to track their time off. Whenever someone has reached 100 percent of his (her) weekly goal and wants to use any or all of his earned time off, simply smile and wave good-bye.

Once again, in an industry where burnout runs high, time off becomes a valuable and desired commodity in any amount. And those of you who have worked on the phone know how true this is. Now if you are still questioning whether you can afford to offer time off, I would suggest that you read this chapter as many times as necessary. If you set up the guidelines as I've outlined here, you can't afford not to give time off.

**Warning:** Absolutely do not even consider reducing an employee's pay for taking his (her) earned time off, regardless of whether he is salaried or paid by the hour. If you make this cat-

astrophic blunder, the whole program will turn counterproductive and its value will fall from diamonds to stone. Imagine
raising someone's quota, inspiring them to work hard to meet
your challenge and then 'rewarding' them with time off work
without pay! This tragic twist is not a reward, and therefore,
not an option. The time-off incentive is strictly a perk, a reward
for over achievement. It is not a disciplinary suspension from
work. Consider it a paid 'mini-vacation.' If the employee
achieves the goal and earns time off, he certainly deserves to
be paid for it.

# 4

# Training

D on't even think about skipping this chapter. Maybe I caught you in the act of thinking, "My people have already been trained." Or maybe you're thinking, "My people know how to do their jobs, they don't need training," or "My employees don't like training."

If you are guilty of one or more of these kinds of thoughts or if you question how training and motivation can be mentioned in the same breath, you've got plenty of company. For reasons I can never figure out, too many managers and supervisors in our industry feel that training their people is one of the lowest tasks on their priority list. Now before you get all riled up and put on the old defensive uniform, let me explain. I'm fairly certain that most of you out there do some kind of training. When you hire someone off the street they may not even know how to spell your company's name. Of course there has to be training involved in any job. I challenge you to look at two simple questions and then answer them honestly. I mean totally honestly. Number one, is your initial training program as complete as it needs to be? And number two, how extensive and diversified are your ongoing training programs? There, that wasn't so hard. Or was it? Let's take a closer look.

While consulting for many companies I have found a number of good initial training programs. But unfortunately that number represents a low percentage. Most programs range from fair down to almost totally inadequate. How critical is this, you may ask. Well, think about it this way. Consider all the time, effort, and money that goes into hiring someone. You write the advertisement, advertise for the job, respond to the incoming calls for the position, review resumes and applications, make phone calls to the applicants to set up interviews, conduct interviews sessions, etc. If you're hiring more than one person multiply this accordingly. The recruiting process eats up a lot of resources and that's one good reason to properly train the people you hire. If you don't, you'll be back to square one sooner than you'd like, going through the same expensive process of recruiting all over again. Does this sound familiar? It does to me. I know how it feels to be a Human Resource hiring machine where your whole life seems to be interviewing or training, and it's not a fun feeling. Years ago I was an assistant telemarketing manager at USA Today where the annual turnover on 100 employees was more than 500%! While hiring and training were part of my responsibilities, they were not supposed to take over my life. It wasn't long before I realized that I was spending all of my time and energy on recruiting. And I decided to do something about it. After careful analysis, I determined that the number one contributor to the turnover problem was lack of training. Through a revised initial training program and additional ongoing training, I was able to reduce the annual turnover in our office by over 400%.

Let's briefly consider some of the necessary components for initial training programs and some training ideas that will help make your programs more successful. The INITIAL TRAINING must include but not be limited to the following:

## 1. Telephone Techniques

Technique is important for both inexperienced and experienced salespeople. While this module of training introduces the how's and why's to the newcomers to our industry, it also acts as a strong refresher course for veterans with any amount of experience.

## 2. Communication Skills

Don't assume that your people already have all the necessary communication skills they'll ever need. Given the requirement of good communication skills in our industry, why would you consider not including this in the initial training program? Let's consider the importance of both presentation skills and listening skills.

The ability to clearly convey the objective of the call with the essential inflection and enthusiasm requires training and attention. Industry research statistics show the following percentage breakdown of communication during a sale:

| Face To Face | | Telephone |
|---|---|---|
| 55% | Body Language | 0% |
| 38% | Tone/Voice | 88% |
| 7% | Words | 12% |

Observe the breakdown for business over the telephone. Success is determined 88% by tone and voice. In other words, it isn't what you say but how you say it. I'm sure you've heard this before, probably many times. And you've probably said this to others. That's because it's true. Remember that if someone doesn't like the way you're saying something, there's a good chance he won't even hear the content of your message. Inflection, personality, excitement and enthusiasm are all essential for successful presentations.

Think about some of the telemarketing calls you've received at home. If you're like me you've heard more than one call where the salesperson is obviously reading to you, using zero enthusiasm and zero inflection. This comes from zero training. People don't want to hear someone read to them over the phone. Years ago I received a call from one of the early automated recorded messages that began (in a monotonous reading tone), "Good evening, Wormans, I'm glad you're home. I have a very important message, here we go." About this time I called for my wife to pick up the other phone and listen to this recorder (or what I thought was a recorder). But the recorder reacted immediately and said, "Mr. Worman, are you still there?" At this point I was thinking, "Wow, this must be voice-activated for response. But then it hit me. The mundane presentation that sounded like a recorder was actually a human being. How embarrassing this was for both of us. The point here is that a lack of enthusiasm, intensity and inflection usually means no success. Maybe you've heard this saying:

People buy only when they understand.
They can understand only what they hear.
They hear only when they listen.
They listen only when they're interested.

Your most important tool for generating interest in the listener is the way you sound.

Listening skills are the most underrated segment of training. This is ironic since research studies show us the following about listening:

- It consumes more waking hours than any other activity.
- After eight hours we forget 50% of what we hear. And after two days we lose 95% unless we can associate it with visual clues.
- The average person listens with only 25% of his or her capacity and only 10% of the brain's memory capacity.
- The average person can speak about 125 words per minute but can hear, listen and think between 400-600 words per minute.
- Listening is the communication skill that we learn first, we use the most, but is taught the least. (How does this make sense?)

In general, most people have poor listening skills no matter how good their hearing is. Hearing and listening are two different things. For fun, try something that I do as part of every training session or consulting assignment to illustrate what lazy listeners most of us are. Take a story from the newspaper and develop seven fairly tough questions about the story. One day without warning, tell your people you want to read a short article from the newspaper. After you read it, ask them to answer a few questions on paper regarding the story you just read. Be prepared. They'll always be shocked, they'll probably grumble and ask you if you're serious. This is natural, since most of them were not interested in your story in the first place. And typically, their minds wandered off to more relevant, personal thoughts instead of paying attention. And suddenly you're going to test them? In front of everyone else? Maybe you're not a very popular person right about now. But proceed to ask your questions as they write down their answers. If you can, walk among them as you ask your questions for a preview of their answers. Following the last question I lighten the mood with something like, "Before anyone decides to run his keys along the side of my car, remember that this quiz is just for fun." Then proceed to ask each question to the group, asking for voluntary answers until you have received an answer to each question. Then ask how many got all seven correct. (I've never seen a hand here.) How many got six correct? (Again, never seen a hand here.) How about five? (You might have a few.) Who got four? (Some more hands.) Stop here before you embarrass anyone and then conclude with something like the following: "Your level of interest in this story is irrelevant here. Prospects and customers often talk about something that is not of great interest to you. If I told you in advance that I was going to read something and then quiz you and that anyone getting all seven correct would win $20, I know I'd be handing out some $20's right now. (You always see people acknowledge that you are correct here.) Now you must remind them that there are dollars at stake every time they pick up the phone. If they're not listening, they will miss buying signals or important information that could otherwise put them in the driver's seat that steers right to the cash register. This is a great exercise that brings some fun to a serious subject. The bottom line is that good listening skills are essential for success in our business. I follow the quiz with some points about common barriers to effective listening as well as proven ways to enhance their listening skills.

Remember that good salespeople are good talkers. But the best salespeople are good listeners. Why do you think God gave us two ears and only one mouth?

### 3. Script Review

Script training is a necessity, especially in your initial training program, no matter what kind of calls your salespeople make. Whether their calls are for research, customer satisfaction, surveys, sales, or lead generation, teaching them the art of delivering the message of your call objective will drive their success. And don't take the easy way out here. Just because you've given them time to read the script or take it home to study doesn't mean you've trained them. This is what we refer to as a self-inflicted wound that's potentially fatal. When new telemarketing people get off to a weak start, turnover is probably right around the corner. The single biggest cause of failure in the early stages of telemarketing is the lack of understanding and practice in using the script or call guide—in other words, a lack of training.

Stop for a minute and analyze how much dedicated time goes into your script training. While you're doing that, I'm going to refer back to my consulting notes to prove the power of proper script training. One company asked me to concentrate my first few days on initial training for their employees who were coming in the front door and leaving through the back door faster than a New York subway turnstile. It took me until about

8:19 a.m. on the first day to figure out that the biggest reason for the high turnover was their mediocre performance level. Very few people understood how to use the script. Unsuccessful people usually become unhappy and unhappy people are usually goners. One of the executives asked me at lunch that day, "Do you think it has something to do with their phone presentations?" As my daughter Jackie would say, "Come 'ere, that deserves a slap." Of course it does! Further investigation showed that their script training involved free time to study the script quietly as well as thirty minutes face-to-face role playing with the other new hires—who also did not know what they were doing yet. The end product was timid employees who were embarrassed to get on the phone in front of others because of their lack of confidence. This lead to turnover and having to start the whole recruiting process again. This entire headache is unnecessary. The following points represent the various phases of script training I have done for my new employees and that I recommend for you.

- Prior to the start date, the employee takes the scripts, call guides, common objections and answers for review and practice.
- I recommend that during all phases of training they spend any spare minutes studying the script.
- Set aside a dedicated time frame for script training. This sets the tone for the importance of this phase of training.
- I open this phase of training with a "verbal walk through" of the script, highlighting the critical areas and emphasizing the importance of personality and enthusiasm.

Maybe you're wondering why I didn't make a tape of this so I don't have to say the same thing every time? I do have cassette tapes but I recommend using these only in your ongoing training or when you absolutely cannot do this segment in person. I have found over the years that the success of communicating the necessary excitement and intensity is far greater when you perform live.

Just a quick thought here. This is usually a good time to review the importance of opening statements, the first 15 seconds or so of your presentation. These 15 seconds comprise the most critical point in your conversation. Always train your people about the two MUST DO's and the four ABSOLUTE DON'T's in the opening of their presentation.

## First let's look at the four ABSOLUTE DON'T's.
### 1. Don't Stumble Over Your Words
Maybe you can't prevent all stumbling even with solid training. Mistakes happen.  However, practice, practice and more practice will certainly raise your odds of making smooth opening statements.

### 2. Don't Have A Paper Fight
When you call people and try to capture their attention, don't let them hear paper shuffling in the background. This annoying sound creates the image of a disorganized person searching for their place in their presentation. A paper fight sounds unprofessional and usually dampens the success of your presentation.

### 3. Don't Become A Radio Announcer
It's a common belief that to command attention on the phone you have to change your voice to the deep, bellowing sound of a disc jockey. During my consulting assignments I spend a block of time monitoring phone calls and listening to presentations. And at almost every company I will encounter someone who subscribes to the radio persona. While monitoring someone I call him in and make a suggestion or two. He goes back to the phone and I continue monitoring except that now I can't find the person I just met with. Maybe his extension changed in the last five minutes or maybe I pushed the wrong button? But then I realize that same person was calling from the same phone but

is now using a different voice. For some reason, when he knows I will be listening to him again, he feels he has to change his voice into Mr. Radio Announcer. This is always a turn-off. When you do something unnatural on the phone, that's exactly how you will sound. Unnatural. Train your people to just be themselves.

## 4. Don't Read It

Remember my story earlier in this chapter about the call that sounded like a recorded message? No one likes to be read to over the phone. And if you put someone to sleep in the first 15 seconds they hang around to listen anyway. Teach your people about the importance of enthusiasm, especially in the opening of every call. If your people are not excited about what they're talking about, none of their prospects will be excited about listening. The more they practice their opening statements, the better their delivery will be.

**Now that we've looked at the four ABSOLUTE DON'T's let's cover the two MUST DO's.**

## 1. Do Sound Confident

Some people ooze with confidence. You know the kind. You can sense it from the minute you see or hear them. Confidence is a wonderful feeling. Think about something you've done in your life or something you're very good at that brings out your feelings of confidence. Think of those times when you're in a discussion about something you know a lot about. Think of that feeling of knowing what you're talking about that brings your enthusiasm to the discussion. This same air of confidence plays a vital role in the success of a phone call, especially in the opening statements. Remember our discussion earlier about the importance of how you say something compared to what you are saying. Your level of confidence during your opening statements can set the tone for success later in the call or set the stage for failure early on.

## 2. Do Create A Solid Opening
## By Choosing The Right Words

Even if your people are confident and enthusiastic, do not underestimate the importance of the actual words in your opening statement. Make sure that the first opening statements get the listener involved in the conversation, that it peaks their interest and causes them to wonder, "What do they have?" or "I need to listen to this." Make sure you caution your people about asking risky questions like "How are you today?" or "How's your day going?" that can kill the sales opportunity before the opening presentation is over. These niceties, commonly known as icebreakers, cause problems because people are not trained to listen to the response and respond to the answer. I have regularly observed poor listening skills and the same improper responses while monitoring conversations during consulting assignments and also during telemarketing calls I get at home. Here's what usually happens:

SALESPERSON:  "This is so and so from ABC company, how are you today?"
PROSPECT:       "Well, I've had better days."
SALESPERSON:  "That's great, the reason for my call . . ."

Stop—put the brakes on! "That's great?" What does that mean? It's great that the prospect is not having a good day? The salesperson is so used to looking at the script and habitually responding "That's great," that he forgets to listen to the person's response. This happens so often that many trainers and managers do not include this question in the script. But instead of eliminating the question, you can prepare your people to respond to it. And no, this doesn't mean saying "I'm sorry," or "That's too bad." While this response may appear to be kind and sensible, it couldn't be further from the appropriate reply. When someone indicates they're not doing well and you say, "I'm sorry but here's my sales pitch," that's insensitive. Another downfall of this response is the subsequent conversation about why the prospect is not doing well. All you've really done here is remind them of their problems and now you're both sitting in the depression. Neither of these responses is appropriate. Instead of "I'm sorry," or "That's too bad," try this: "I'm glad I called because I'm gonna brighten your day." This type of upbeat response will spin them off in a positive direction. You need to change their day from bad to good, not help them bathe in their tears.

Finally, be careful not to sabotage your opening statements and kill your sales opportunity. This sabotage happens throughout our industry everyday. People are sabotaging their own calls before they get a chance to start. Let me give you some examples to give you a feel for what I'm talking about. The names have been changed to protect the guilty.

■ "Is Mr. Smith available, or is he busy?"

What do you think happened here and what do you suppose the response will be? You're right, Mr. Smith is suddenly busy. Let's look at another one:

■ "Is Mrs. Jones in or is this a bad time?"

Well, what happened here? You're right again. It probably will be a bad time. Here's one more, and this one nearly gave me a coronary attack:

■ "May I please speak with Bill or is he doing something important?"

Aaahhh! Is he doing something important? What is that? What does that say about your call? It says that what you're calling about it is not important. It also conveys a lack of confidence and professionalism.

These examples illustrate the act of butchering the opening statements, which in turn signs the death warrant to the phone call. When you give screeners this kind of option, you always lose. Screeners are already good at what they do. Don't make their job any easier. A bad opening presents a challenging—if not impossible—recovery. If you stumble in the beginning, you won't even get the chance to close your prospect.

Now that we've looked at opening statements let's move on to script training. Employees should now be separated into pairs for practicing role-play. The amount of time needed depends on the complexity of your presentation. If you've only hired one person, select one of your best current employees to role play, or do what I do—do it yourself. These sessions should not be done sitting face to face and practicing back and forth. You want to stay closer to reality. The more realistic the setting, the better. Did you ever play army as a kid? My brothers and I always tried to look like TV's Sergeant Saunders from Combat. Remember Vic Morrow as the cool and tough Sarge? We used to fight over who would get the plastic machine gun because this determined who would most look like Saunders. Why did it matter so much? Because the more authentic you feel, the more you get into whatever you're doing. This is no different with industry role-play. After teaming the people in pairs, put them on phones as far away from each other as possible so they can feel more realistic about these simulated calls.

I conduct a final group session as I play the role of the customer. One at a time each person takes a turn going back to the sales division to phone us in the conference room. Then he makes his presentation to me over the speakerphone with all of the other new hires listening. Playing the role of the tough customer, I toss out every possible objection as the salesperson tries to sell me the product. Is this too hard on the new hires, you wonder? Doesn't it intimidate and embarrass them? Isn't it cruel and unnecessary punishment? To answer your question, yes. And no. Yes, they're probably nervous, intimidated and even embarrassed. And no, this is not punishment. In fact, this crucial aspect of script training is the best technique for preparing your new hires for live calls. During these role-play calls, I stop and talk with the employee about ways to improve, thus training everyone at once. When a question arises, everyone benefits from the discussion about the concerns and solutions. A softer approach would only set up your trainees for sales suicide. You'll mislead them into thinking that everyone will buy or least be nice to them, or for that matter, even listen to their presentation. Trust me, it doesn't happen this way. What I'm doing prepares them for what they're really going to face so we can learn how to react and respond before it happens. If you cut corners when it comes to script training, the only thing you're really cutting is your own throat.

### 4. Objections/Answers

While proper script training is imperative for your initial training programs, it only works if you allow enough time for your employees to understand the prospect's objections and learn to respond to them. It's like peanut butter and jelly. If you put the peanut butter or the jelly alone on a sandwich it's okay but not real good. When you put them together you have a powerful combination. Likewise, this training segment is essential for the success of your people. Let's consider the concept of objections. Most people in our industry think that objections are a negative reaction that you must learn to overcome or even avoid. That's why so many people in our industry are afraid of objections. The truth is, there is no reason to be frightened of

49

something that can prove to be a sales resource. That's right, objections can help you, but only if you understand them in their true light. When we finish this part of training together I hope you will see objections for what they really are—buying signals! Let's look at the following definitions of objections:

### Objections from the prospect are defined as follows:

- a symptom of their lack of complete and accurate information
- their misunderstanding of the information you presented
- a strong emotional stance that may or may not be related to the aforementioned—it might be illogical
- your misunderstanding of what they want
- a genuine problem they are having with your offer
- Most importantly, objections are the prospect's way of letting you know they require additional information before they can buy.

Say that last point again, along with me: Objections are the prospect's way of letting you know that they require additional information before they can buy. Therefore objections are buying signals, right? Absolutely. And if they're buying signals, why is everyone so panic-stricken about them? I'll tell you why. They probably will have objections to buying. Most phone calls to prospects and even customers will include objections from the other end of the phone. So what? Many sales begin when the customer says no. And many sales happen when the customer says no more than once. In fact studies show that 40% of your telemarketing success will happen after multiple no's. Forty percent. This suggests the importance of training employees in responding to objections, doesn't it? Now that we agree on that, let's dissect some objections and find out what we're really dealing with.

Always teach your employees about the standard reasons for objecting, fondly known as the **four P's:**

1. **P**roduct/Service • they don't need it.
2. **P**ostponement • time must pass before they can speak with you again or buy.
3. **P**ersonal • they hold something against you or your company.
4. **P**rice • product/service cost is too high, no budget, etc.

You must then discuss each objection as it applies to your specific product or service. And don't fall for the decoys, objections that are only a smoke screen. Industry studies show over and again that more than 50% of the first objections are not real. The prospect just wants to get you off of the phone. You must train your salespeople to at least get through the first objection and uncover the real reason that the prospect is saying no. Then use the following **four-step process to answer objections**.

### 1. Cushion The Prospect/Customer

Use softening statements like "I understand," or "I see." The best softening statement I ever heard or used is "Let's talk about that." This statement shows your interest in your prospect's concern and your willingness to address it. When you cushion your prospect with softening statements, you are verbally putting your arm around him.

### 2. Isolate The Primary Objection

Using the simple skills of probing, questioning and good listening, you can uncover the real concern by answering all of his decoys, asking the right questions and listening to what he says.

### 3.Answer The Objection With Benefits

Excite the prospect or customer with the benefits of your product or service.

### 4.Close Again

No matter how well you do the three other things, if you don't close again, you've wasted your time and effort. And believe it or not, this happens a lot. I can't tell you how many thousands of times I've heard this while monitoring my own people and during consulting assignments. They cushion the prospect, identify the objections, answer them with benefits and then . . . and then . . . go brain-dead. They don't close again. In case you missed the latest telemarketing news flash, "the sale isn't coming to you, you need to go after it!" The next session looks more deeply into THE CLOSE.

Objections can be a nightmare to many people. Just as you would comfort a child having a nightmare, comfort your employees by showing them there's no reason to be frightened.

If your salespeople understand what objections are really about and they're prepared with good, strong responses, they will be far less afraid of them and therefore, more successful.

### 5. Company Orientation

How much do your employees know about the company they work for? Unfortunately, the typical answer is "not too much" or a sarcastic "enough," or something indicating that the employees don't need to know about the company, only about the job. My question is why?

Granted, it is not necessary for most employees to have access to confidential information, financial documentation or certain strategic forecasting. But are your people even aware of how your department interfaces with other divisions or what process takes place after their success on the telephone? If so, I commend you. If not, here comes a rope, latch on!

Most employees are interested (sometimes too much) in the inner workings of their employer company. And why not? I am, aren't you? The special feature about this training module is that a little bit goes a long way, usually. While there will always be a few people who test your last nerve with truckloads of questions that you never thought of asking, most people will be content with a small piece of company history, background, current status and future outlook. This knowledge makes people feel more secure and confident.

Did you ever ask people about their work and their company, only to sense some discomfort followed by a vague response? For example, someone might say "Well, we distribute this," or "We manufacture that," or worse, "Our division is responsible for . . ." meaning they can't tell you much about the rest of the company. I'm not talking about having the inside scoop on everyone's lives or being a major player on the gossip team but having a general knowledge of the company, its mission, and how it operates. Not only is this not bad or dangerous, it's healthy. And in many cases it helps your telephone professionals do a better job. Even if your company contracts third party service doing specialized telemarketing projects for others, it is valuable for the employees on each project to understand at least a little bit about the company, above and beyond the objective of the call.

This portion of my training always comes first. It seems to help the newly hired employees acclimate faster. And the faster they feel comfortable the more attention they'll pay to the rest of your training. Think about that. If their minds are busy wandering and wondering, their attention will be constantly distracted instead of following you. A new job is among the Top 10 stressful situations, so do what you can to ease the strain during an already difficult time.

The advantage in this segment of training is that you can easily get help with it. If you can set up a meeting schedule with the department heads of all other divisions and lock in the time frames. The employees will visit from one department to the next for thirty to sixty minutes of education about each area.

Will they retain it all? Of course not, but that's okay. Most will jot down notes, ask questions and leave each area with a general understanding of each department's function within the company. More knowledge will naturally come later but this initial exposure puts them in a general comfort zone about the company for whom they've selected to work. First, they are now prepared to answer the inevitable barrage of questions that awaits them when they get home. And second, they are at least informed enough to sound reasonably knowledgeable when they first go live on the phone. It is also helpful to include company history documentation with the introductory pack that you give your new hires.

The bottom line is that most people are interested in learning more about their employer company. If they are interested, don't make them live in a departmental vacuum without knowledge of the very corporation or project they represent. And if they're not interested, a big old red flag just went up, and that's not a good sign. I smell a turnover in the oven.

### 6. The Secrets of Effective Telemarketing

While there are probably a million and one little secrets to selling by phone, I suggest that in your initial training you touch on the following **TOP 10 essentials for any hope of success.** This also makes a useful checklist for veterans in your ongoing training programs.

**1. Know your objective before you make the call.**
Don't assume that your people really understand the objective of their calls. The typical vague understanding will not be enough to close the deal. It is crucial that they clearly understand the intended result every time they dial.

There should always be more than one objective to each call. Obviously, your number one goal is across-the-board success: the sale, the completed survey; the appointment or whatever total success means in your environment. But is the call considered a failure if ultimate success is not achieved? Absolutely not. In fact, I don't even like the word failure. Teach your people that every call is a success, but at different levels. If the ultimate success is not achieved, make sure you are successful at gathering important information. What is the name of the decision-maker? When will he return? What is the best time to reach him? When looking at this information as a secondary objective, you can make every call a success. And remember, today's no can be tomorrow's yes, so your success in gathering this critical information will mean a better chance for success later.

## 2. Have all the materials you need before you make the call.

Organization is what we're talking about here. Have your script or presentation guide, product information, answers to objections, and all necessary materials at your fingertips and in view. Your presentation will not be professional if you have to put your prospect on hold to look for something or if you're shuffling through papers for something that should have been at your fingertips. Good preparation and basic organization will simply result in greater success.

## 3. Identify yourself whether you are calling the customer or the customer is calling you.

Introduction is a general etiquette that's often forgotten. Most people want to know who is speaking to them and not by just the first name. While identification may seem insignificant, don't be fooled. Remember the importance of those first 15 seconds? The introduction of your name will certainly be within that time frame. Identifying yourself will also make your prospect or customer feel more at ease. Rushing through your introduction or using first name only can give your customer an uncomfortable feeling about the call.

### 4. Speak clearly and emphasize key words and phrases.

How are people going to be interested in what your employees have to say if they can't even understand what they are saying? Remember our earlier discussion about the importance of good communication skills. Important is an understatement. Communication is imperative. We're not in the "teleconning" business where you don't want prospects and customers to understand what you're presenting. I'm not suggesting we go back to our first grade reading exercises and exaggerate clear diction. ("See Ted run. Watch Sally play.") But speaking clearly means a smoother presentation and this will obviously help the prospect understand what you are calling for. Once again, this means a higher success rate no matter what the call objective.

While emphasis can be valuable, too much emphasis is . . . well, too much. Overemphasis reminds us of the infomercial guy at 3:00 a.m., the guy with the tie that stops about halfway down his stomach, the guy who's screaming about "three easy payments," "no risk, no obligation" and other sales speak phrases.

On the other hand, key words and phrases need inflection or they will blend in with the rest of the presentation and lose their punch. You can use emphasis and inflection for a more enthusiastic, potentially successful presentation, or a mundane monotone presentation for a boring script reading that nobody wants to hear. The choice is yours.

### 5. Block out external distractions.

This precaution sounds deceptively easier than it really is. As members of the human race, distractions are part of life. The point is that we shouldn't allow them to control our day or the outcome. This is one of the keys to becoming and remaining successful in our industry. If something negative happened before you left for work or something good was happening that night after work, you've got to make sure it doesn't interfere with your workday. External also means internal when referring to office distractions. Nearby conversations, office gossip, employee disagreements and other internal activities are also considered external distractions.

Simply put, anything that diverts your employees' attention away from their job would be considered an external distraction. Allowing any of these situations to interfere with productivity can be devastating. One of your managerial responsibilities is to help your people concentrate on their jobs by creating an environment where positivity is the norm and focusing is as easy as possible.

Like death and taxes, distractions are a certainty. They will happen. You can choose to ignore them and suffer the consequences or help your employees understand how to offset them. Don't make the mistake of omitting this subject in training. If you do, you're avoiding reality.

## 6. Use short sentences and language appropriate to your customer.

Many people in our industry mistakenly feel that if they extend their sentences with words that need to be measured in feet, they can schmooze and woo the prospect into closing. And others buy the theory that industry jargon will impress the prospect into a sale. Forget that idea. Train your people that using short sentences and language that your customer understands is more professional and actually increases their chances for success. I know we mentioned this earlier but it merits repeating:

"People buy only when they understand.

They can understand only what they hear.

They hear only when they listen.

They listen only when they're interested."

A prospect is not going to buy unless he listens and understands. He won't understand and probably won't even listen if your people are trying to impress him with abbreviations, industry slang and complicated verbosity (!) about what you are marketing. Simple is better. This ill-fated attempt to impress customers is a double loss. Your customers won't be impressed and neither will the boss when he sees the low rate of success.

**7. If you don't know the answer, admit it and get back to your customer later with the information.** Oh boy, here's a doozy. Get ready to attack your employees in one of the most vulnerable areas known to man, the ego. In this case, bursting their bubbles is inevitable. They must hear, understand and accept that they don't know everything and that it's fine to tell a prospect or customer that they will have to get back to them later with an answer. It's almost like Fonzie (from the old 70's sitcom Happy Days) who just couldn't say, "I was wrong." Remember how he'd try over and over but it would come out, "I was wr . . ." He just couldn't spit out those words. For some reason, many people consider it a negative to say, "I don't know." Why? Here's where I have to say, "I don't know." Let's look at the alternative which usually includes speculation, guesswork, fabrication or in some cases a combination of all three.

Has this happened to you like it has to me? Someone calls you and during the conversation you ask a question, only to hear a perplexed voice that responds with something like "Well if I had to guess, I would say this," or "I'm not sure but let's go with this." Talk about a confidence buster! "If I had to guess?" What's that? I didn't ask for a guess, I want the right answer. If you're not sure, why don't you get sure by asking someone who knows. I would much rather hear, "I don't know the answer to that but I will find out, can you hold on or should I call you back?" Probably you would too. Most people would. Your employees need to know that they won't know the answers to all the questions and that's all right. But don't invent a problem by faking, guessing, speculating or fabricating information because you're afraid to admit ignorance. Your customer will appreciate the correct answer even if it means a short wait. If you don't believe this, think back to the last time you asked for directions and heard, "Well, let's see, I think you go down to the next light and no, maybe it's two lights down. Yeah, then you turn down the fourth or fifth street on your left after that light, or is it on the right? No, I think it's on the left. Then you're going to pass a—wait a minute. I've got a shortcut for you." You get my point, right?

**8. Focus on the needs of your customer.**
At the risk of sounding like "Telemarketing 101," do not assume that your employees are always focusing on the needs of your customers. Too many other things tend to distort one's vision, most of all selfishness. Naturally, employees are just people and they're going to have other agendas such as, "How much commission will I make if I get this sale?" or "One more sale and I get to go home early for the weekend." There's a wide range of self-directed thoughts that keep your employees from concentrating on the most important factor, the customer's needs. But here's the bottom line. Have you noticed that the employees who concentrate on the customers' needs are more successful? No, it's not an accident and it isn't luck. The more you concentrate on the prospect's needs, the more you will understand them, thereby increasing your chance for success.

I once had a door-to-door 'box vendor' come to my office selling overhead pictures of Cleveland's Municipal Stadium, home of the Indians and Browns. They were beautiful and so I entertained his pitch to sell me one. It was a weak presentation but I stuck it out until he closed me with "So, would you like one for $49.95?" My response was simple and honest: "I love the picture. I want to talk to my wife about it over lunch, could you stop by tomorrow?" Even with 20-200 vision, the guy should have seen the sale. I gave him plenty of verbal and emotional buying signals. Anyway, what followed was the single worst example I've seen of not focusing on the customer's needs. He replied, "Well, I guess I won't reach my quota today." I couldn't believe my ears! He could have said, "Great, what time is good tomorrow?" or "Would you like me to leave the picture here so you can show her?" or any response indicating that he even cared what was important to me. The only thing that was clouding up his selfish mind was his own quota. Worse than that, he tried to play the old guilt trip game on me for his own benefit. As he left I couldn't help thinking to myself, "You're right about one thing, buddy. You're probably not going to reach your quota today or tomorrow or maybe not ever. If he had focused on my needs, he would have made a sale. Needless to say, I didn't buy the picture. I was so turned off by his selfishness that the picture suddenly didn't look so beautiful. The same will happen with your product if your people are not trained to concentrate on the needs of the customers instead of their own. And remember that by focusing on the needs of your customer, most of your own needs will be taken care of too.

### 9. Be honest.

We don't need to elaborate much on this subject. There is no compromise, no middle ground. You can't be "a little bit pregnant." Either you are or you aren't. Either you're honest or you're not. But I can tell you this: unethical sales tactics, fibbing, and little white lies will only bring disaster. Unhappy customers, lack of respect and confidence in your company and a negative gossip line to your other customers will inevitably surface. Let's just live by what mom and dad always taught us, "Honesty is the best policy."

## 10. Thank your customer for his or her time and business.

This practice should go without saying. Unfortunately, it doesn't. Whether you actually get the sale, the appointment, the lead, or the completed survey, it is proper etiquette to thank the person on the other end. Remember that today's no is tomorrow's yes. If you do not follow etiquette, today's no will be tomorrow's no and probably a no forever.

While the previous ten tips may seem obvious, they are abused and butchered everyday in our industry. When you train people on the importance of these Top 10 you create a more positive and productive environment, and that means more motivated employees.

## 7. Product Or Service Training

Obviously, your employees should have a complete understanding about the product or service that you are offering over the phone. Be careful not to under-train them. Too often employees have insufficient knowledge, which can only lead to less confidence, less calls, less success, and too often, "less employees." For your people to feel confident in their presentation and how they will deal with objections, they must own full knowledge of your product or service. Giving them materials to look through at home may be a good start but it's hardly enough. Be sure to follow this with a question-answer session. This will ensure that all of the trainees can address their concerns and feel comfortable about the product or service your company offers. Obviously, this isn't rocket science. The better informed your salespeople, the more likely they are to make more calls, give better presentations, close more sales, sell

61

more products, feel more successful and ultimately, stay on the job longer. Is there any further discussion necessary?

## 8. Effective Probing

This valuable technique usually gets too little time and attention. What's so valuable about probing, you ask? Asking good questions accomplishes the following goals:
- It helps you gather important information.
- It helps you determine what motivates the prospect to buy.
- It helps you uncover the prospect's real objections.

If you don't ask questions, you are making an announcement to an unqualified suspect. Probing with questions turns suspects into prospects. It also helps eliminate some objections before they ever occur.

Train your people to preface questions with, "Let me ask you this." When someone knows that a question is coming, they will more often be in a listening mode, and we have already established the importance of good listening skills. It's a proven fact that the person who is asking the right questions is usually in control of the conversation and often the outcome.

## 9. Call Reluctance

I'm probably one of the few people who believe you should address this problem before it happens. It will happen, so better to train people to identify the symptoms so they can deal with the problem before it gets worse. This is preventative maintenance, pure and simple. If you don't put oil in your car, you're going to have engine problems sooner or later. And those problems will get worse and worse until the final breakdown. Then it's too late; you need a new car. If you don't train your people about call reluctance, some will have sales blocks sooner or later and they will get worse and worse until a final breakdown occurs. Then it's too late; you need a new employee. Help yourself, your new employees, and ultimately your company by training your employees about call reluctance.

First, let's identify what this means. Call reluctance is the dreaded disease that attacks almost everyone in the telemarketing and telesales industry at one time or another. It comes in different ways, shapes and forms but carries the same punch. It kills your call volume. Call reluctance is easy to recognize if you know what you're looking for: too many trips to the restroom, organizing, reorganizing and re-reorganizing your desk area, looking through your leads over and over again, etc. When someone doesn't want to make calls, they will find a multitude of things to do—anything other than making a call. While we certainly don't know all the reasons why call reluctance strikes, I can tell you the top two: **fear of rejection** and **fear of objections.** With this in mind, we can diminish the chances of it occurring by educating people about both causes.

### 1. Fear of Rejection

No one likes to be rejected. But being afraid of rejection is a different matter. In a training session, always find out what your salespeople are afraid of. Ask them to tell you the worst thing that could happen when they make a call. Whenever I ask that question to new employees, I always get the same answers. "Someone could yell or cuss at you," or "someone may hang up on you." You're right, they might. And your point is . . .? My point is, so what? Big deal. If that's the worst that could happen, that's not so bad. Everything short of that can't be too terrible, right? Prepare your people for the worst that could happen and everything else will seem insignificant, especially when the worst thing isn't so bad.

Also, let's mention what is affectionately known in our business as rejectionitis. This means you call someone and before you can say your name or the name of your company they say, "No, I'm not interested." This really irritates me. How can someone not be interested when they don't even know who you are or why you're calling. I'll bet I'm not alone about what I wanted to say when this used to happen to me. Since I can't put it in print, let me tell you about one of my past employees who took care of all of our frustrations in one call. On behalf of all of us who have ever felt the anger and frustration of rejectionitis, he took care of it.

I was monitoring sales calls one day and decided to monitor one of my better salespeople to gather some training tips. On the first call I heard him get nailed with the old "No, I wouldn't be interested," immediately following his introduction. Without hesitation he replied, "Well, I'm sorry then, you would have been our one millionth sale and the winner of our one million dollar giveaway. But since you're not interested, we'll call someone else. The guy on the other end of the phone started screaming, "No, wait a minute, please wait a minute," and then my employee hung up on him. Picture this poor man screaming and pleading for another chance. He gets hung up on and now has to deal with the fact that if he had only listened for another moment he would be a millionaire. After ten years, this fellow is probably still muttering to himself about his loss. Naturally, I pulled my employee into the office to reprimand him for his unacceptable behavior on the phone. But before I could say anything we both burst out laughing, realizing that he had done what all of us had wanted to do at one time or another, torture someone for rejectionitis. It all boils down to perception. And it's up to you and me as to how our salespeople perceive things.

## 2. Fear of Objections
The only reason people fear objections is if they don't know how to deal with them. If you go back several pages and use that information in your training about how to answer

objections, this cause of call reluctance will almost disappear. Teach your people to understand objections and give them the resources to address them. Remember what fear really is: False Evidence Appearing to be Real.

## 10. Closing skills

Think about all the previous stages of initial training up to this point. You've given your new hires an understanding of your company and its infrastructure. You've trained them on your products or service sales skills, communication skills, telephone techniques, script presentation and how to answer objections. A lot of work, a lot of preparation, a lot of knowledge . . . a lot of wasted time, unless you're going to teach them how to close sales.

I've heard hundreds of people and thousands of presentations that sound strong and enthusiastic but lead nowhere simply because the person doesn't close the sale. He didn't get the commitment. This often happens because he is afraid to close. And this fear comes from not knowing how to close. I also believe that many people in our industry overcomplicate and incorrectly perceive what the close is. Closing is an invitation to do business, nothing more, nothing less. Too many people feel that closing has to be pushy. If you're trying to cram something down someone's throat, you won't be successful. Inviting people to do business with you in a controlled, aggressive way means using good closing techniques.

Most importantly, teach your people to assume the sale. I know I said you shouldn't assume anything. This is true, until the sale. While you're never going to sell everyone, you will sell a much higher percentage of prospects when you assume the sale. First, it's an attitude, believing with confidence before the call, while you're dialing, and during the presentation that you will be successful. Secondly, and equally important, it means presenting yourself well and then verbally assuming the sale.

Letting the prospect know what's going to happen and telling them what's going to happen, not asking. I can't tell you how many thousands of weak closes I have heard over the years. Closes such as "Would you like to try one?" or "Would you like to give it a chance?" or "Could I maybe interest you in our product?" are feeble attempts that will only leave your people unsuccessful, frustrated, de-motivated, and ultimately looking for other employment. But it doesn't have to be this way if you train them in the art of assuming the sale. While some people may grasp this concept quickly, repetitive role-playing may be necessary for others. And be prepared, even with extensive training some may never get it.

While there are many guidelines to closing sales, let's examine the **Five Golden Rules for closing** that I consider imperative for training.

### 1. Always Be Intent On Closing.

Always listen for buying signals. Remember our earlier discussion about the importance of good listening skills? Here's where listening becomes so important. Prospects will often give buying signals that salespeople miss because they weren't listening. When you hear a buying signal, close the sale. Otherwise you'll be feeling obliged to finish going through the script even though you don't need to. It's like not being ready to close even though the customer is. Show your people examples of this during role-play sessions and it will help them understand how to pick up on buying signals so they can close the sale.

### 2. Be Quiet.

The expression silence is golden is especially true in the sales close. Teach your people that after closing a sale they should then close their mouths. This is not the time to talk. Now is the time to listen and then respond. And if there seems to be an endless silence, just be patient. You've just completed a presentation to this person and thrown an opportunity at him. Give him a chance to think about it before he responds. Don't be intimidated by that momentary silence. It's okay. Don't start filling it with more sales tactics because you feel impatient. The prospect must respond with something before you can proceed. If it's yes, finish it off and move on. If it's no, it's time to find out why. If your people get uncomfortable or intimidated by this brief silence and begin to fill it with more sales tactics, their success is headed for a serious decline.

### 3. Close Multiple Times If the Prospect is Saying No.

Research shows that 40% of telemarketing success is generated after the prospect has said no more than once. You must prepare your people for multiple rejection. Train them to close multiple times in any situation that allows for it. Do you have any of those people that believe their odds are better with the next call, so they think it's better to move on after one no? Yeah, I've had those too. The key word here is had. First, probably the most difficult task in our industry is reaching the decision-maker, the person you need to speak with. Once you've got him why would you let him off the phone after one no? Second, we've already established that 40% of sales success happens after multiple rejection. Can your employee, you, or your company afford to lose 40% of those sales? I don't think so. Third and finally, think of the leads that are literally being wasted by an individual who refuses to close more than once. Enough said. Teach your people about the financial rewards when they get in the habit of closing multiple times whenever possible.

## 4. Use Every Objection as an Opportunity to Close.

Remember what we discussed earlier about the percentage of sales that occur after multiple no's? It's 40%. So it goes without saying that much of your people's success will come by being mentally prepared and having the resources to answer objections (many more times than once) on any given call. Anytime you get an objection, you need to go through the four-step process we talked about earlier in this chapter, with a slight emphasis on step number four: close again. You must close your prospect each and every time an objection comes up. Make sure your people see it as an opportunity and not a chore.

## 5. When the Sale is Made Terminate the Call.

It is crucial that we train our people to not oversell, to not drift into other subject matter that is not relevant to the objective of your call. Over the years I have heard count-less sales go sour because the salesperson decided to con-tinue the conversation and he literally talked his way right back out of the sale. It happens in many ways. The prospect can change his mind during the extended time; a small-talk topic can upset the prospect into changing his mind, etc. This fatal mistake can happen so easily and strike so quick-ly. I performed this self- inflicted sales butchery one time and one time only.  Let me share the story and the pain.

My job at that time was to set up appointments over the phone for the outside sales reps and the VP of Sales for our company. I had tried for over two months to reach the buyer for a major hotel chain based in Seattle, Washington, to set up an appointment for my boss, our VP of Sales. Finally, I reached the buyer (after some 50 attempts) and presented the benefits of this appointment to discuss our product line in conjunction with their needs. I put a solid close on him and got the appointment! Was I ecstatic or what? My boss had been asking me every week, "Did you reach that hotel chain yet? This would be a great account." Wait until I gave him the news today! My mind was racing as I wound down the particulars: my commission, my happy boss, how persistence had paid off, and other selfish thoughts, when I suddenly went brain dead. Instead of ending the conversation, I asked him how the Seattle Seahawks were doing. Sounds totally innocent, right? It could have started out that way. But within 45 seconds I realized my mistake and within two minutes the error reached total disaster. To make a long story short, the man was a diehard Seahawks fan and a season ticket holder. He did not like my hometown Cincinnati Bengals because of a past incident between the two teams. I didn't find this out until we had talked about the fact that I had been a Public Relations manager for some of the Bengal players (one of which he did not like). At that time, I was still negotiating annual shoe contracts for that player. That tragic two minutes seemed like an eternity as I realized my mistake and unsuccessfully attempted to weasel my way out of it. It ended with him canceling the appointment and hanging up on me! OOOHH, it still hurts! Can you imagine that moment? After months of calling, after finally reaching him, after getting the appointment, after all of that it was over that quick because I didn't get out of the call when the sale was made. Needless to say it was an embarrassing day when I had to report to my boss on the status of that hotel chain.

You are unaware of your prospect's views on most issues so don't take a chance. Teach your employees why they should not drift into unrelated subject matter and teach them not to do it. When the sale is made simply terminate, don't ask how the Seahawks are doing.

And get your people to look forward to closing rather than being afraid of it. That's up to you or the person in charge of training them. Remember that closing is simply an invitation to do business.

## 11. Ongoing Training

I know what you're thinking about now after all this initial training. I can picture the scene: you're propped in your chair, half-reclining (sleeves rolled up and tie loosened if you're a guy), feeling physically and mentally exhausted. You wipe your brow and let out a big sigh thinking, "That's a lot of work, I'm glad training is over." Yes, training is hard work and it can be exhausting. But it's far from over. Structured ongoing training programs are just as important as the initial training process. After all, even the finest automobiles in the world need a regular tune-up.

## Tune-up sessions

Let's consider the car analogy again. Think about how much better your car runs when you change the oil and tune it regularly. Regular maintenance makes a lot more sense than waiting for your car to break down on the side of the road before you have it checked. Maintenance is the key word here. Don't let your employees have a complete breakdown before you look at them. Training is maintenance, a necessary and important maintenance. Tune-up sessions do not have to be extensive or time-consuming. They can be as simple as a 15- or 30-minute quick-hit session at a scheduled time every week or two. You can hold brown-bag luncheons where the employees bring their lunch to work and attend mini seminars during lunchtime. Tune-up sessions should include topics like script review, telephone techniques, communication skills, general sales skills, updated product/service knowledge, and . . . wait a minute. Do these subjects sound familiar? Of course, they're part of your initial training. All you need by way of preparation is to highlight points from any of these issues, grab a few critical seg-

70

ments and you're ready for a tune-up session. If it sounds too easy, you're right, it is. You won't need any major preparation to offer these ongoing sessions that will keep your salespeople in fine operating condition.

Another valuable form of ongoing training is what I call self-improvement training. I use a variety of high-energy, motivational audiotapes on subjects such as setting and achieving goals, positive self-esteem, being a winner, the importance of positive attitude, and many other self-development topics. I have dubbed copies for each master and have broken people into teams for this type of training. The process is simple. Each team gets a different tape on a Monday (team members get copies of the same tape but all teams are working on a different tape). Give them a week or ten days to listen to the tape several times and have them fill out a brief questionnaire about their reaction. Then hold a 15- to 20-minute power session with each team and let them share their thoughts about the tape. This allows everyone to get involved and benefit from each subject. As you go through a series of these (I usually run these four to five times a year for six weeks), you will find that people become more energized, productive and successful. In case you're wondering, you're right, some people may not be interested. They might not listen to the tapes or participate in the sessions. And that's okay. This comes with the job of managing the masses. But you can make the form mandatory so that everyone is required to make an effort. And who knows, people may learn something from their half-hearted effort or from someone else during the participation session. Ultimately, most of your people will benefit from this form of training and will look forward to future sessions.

Another form of ongoing training that I recommend is to set up a mini library in your department. In my library, I include sales and marketing magazines, books, and audio and video-tapes. The subject matter ranges from sales tips to stress management to relationship building. I have coded each library piece with an inventory number and I store everything in a lateral file. I keep a simple log and whenever someone wants to check out something to read or view, they sign the log, I date it, and they return the piece in two weeks. By doing this, you are giving your people the opportunity to improve their personal and professional life on a continuing basis. And of course, you can add to your library whenever you find something worthwhile. Whenever you add a new piece, issue an employee announcement so that everyone will know.

Starting a library does involve some initial cost. But when it comes to good training, the time and money involved is a small investment when you consider the return. And remember that a well-trained employee is a more successful employee and, without question, a more motivated one. Whatever training you do and however you do it, initial and ongoing training are not luxuries or options. Training is a necessity—unless, of course, you don't care about having a more productive environment and positive, motivated employees.

# 5

# Gags and Gimmicks

T hose of you who have attended my seminars and presentations over the years have observed the toy store I carry with me because of my enthusiasm for these symbolic rewards. By far, gags and gimmicks are my favorite non-monetary motivators. Why? There are two reasons. First, these small, playful gestures are fun. And remember we've already established there's nothing wrong with having some fun on the job. In fact, I'm convinced that generating a certain amount of fun in the workplace is healthy. The second reason is that these effective motivators are easy to create. With a little imagination, you can collect a variety of these low-cost items that actually increase performance and productivity.

Unbelievable as it may seem, I have found over the years that this form of recognition is far more gratifying than even cash bonuses. That's right, more popular than the old liquid itself. Part of the reason is visibility—to peers, colleagues and families, as well as to the recipient. Some of these gifts have long-lasting value because they have become treasured keepsakes. Let me share some of my own ideas of the effective gags and gimmicks I have used. Keep in mind as you go read these that not all of them are appropriate to all work environments. But many of the following motivators can work in your department if you're willing to implement them. You will need to be the judge.

## RUBBER WHALE
### . . . for a *whale* of a performance.

You can purchase rubber whales at most toy stores and use them as recognition of a strong performance. You can reward daily performance or give away one or two every week. On the white bottom of each whale, I always write a nice message with a Sharpie marker. The message includes some recognition of the employee's performance, the date and my signature. This makes the reward more of a personal keepsake.

## CALIFORNIA RAISIN
### . . . for employees who are *raisin* their productivity or performance levels by the highest percentage.

Remember this little guy? Years ago you couldn't go any-where without seeing some promotion using the California raisin. The small raisin figurines became very popular. And when they were widely available I bought dozens of them for about one dollar each. You can still find these if you look around. Design a monthly or quarterly program where the employee with the highest percentage of raisin' his performance level or productivity receives one of these awards. I usually mount them on a small wooden block (a trophy shop charges about five dollars). This way they'll stand up and are more likely to wind up on people's desks or workstations, visible for everyone to admire and desire. Employees will work surprisingly hard to receive this little six-dollar item because of its perceived value. The cost of the raisin is irrelevant. It's the status of receiving it that makes it valuable.

## CARDBOARD STARS
### . . . for a *star-studded* performance.

Stars are inexpensive and they deliver such a strong mes-sage. You can purchase them in multiple numbers at party supply store in vivid colors such as blue, red, silver and gold.

Because they're inexpensive, you can give these out more often than some of the other awards. You can use them spontaneously or create a program with guidelines that earn stars. Once again, sign each one with a message to increase its value and watch the collections begin. Do you remember collecting things when you were young? Each kid wanted to outdo the others. If you collected marbles, you wanted more shooters and puries than your friends had. If baseball cards were your thing, you wanted more Mantles and Clementes than anyone else. If you had Barbie dolls, you were determined to have a better wardrobe than your friends had. Guess what? It's no different with these simple little cardboard stars. Everyone wants to collect as many as possible. Why? They symbolize success. Did you ever see college football players with stickers all over their helmets? These represent so many tackles or touchdowns. These stars work the same way. Employees will collect and display them proudly—which turns into ongoing stimulation.

## RECORD
### . . . plastic replica of photographic records for employees who set a *new record* in any productivity category.

This is one of the easiest, least expensive and most effective

motivators I have ever used. When an individual sets a new record for sales volume, appointments, leads, completed surveys or whatever your success is measured by, there's already stimulation involved and recognition attached, as long

75

as you make sure of it. Now let's put the icing on the cake by giving the employee a permanent reminder of their accomplishment, one that will create ongoing motivation: a record. You can buy plastic replicas of 45-RPM records at party supply stores in packs of three for less than $3. They're about eight to ten inches wide, allowing plenty of room to add your personal touch. Write a brief message from you, their leader, congratulating them on their achievement, along with the date and their record-breaking accomplishment.

### And here are two other ideas that work well.

**1.** You can buy oversized plastic replica records just like the little ones. These are a little more expensive but lend themselves to rewarding group performance. When a team of people or your whole department sets a new performance record, you can present this giant record to them and then put it up somewhere visible in your area. As with the smaller records, personalize it by writing the name of the recipient, the performance level achieved and the date. Then find a good place to hang it.

**2.** If a team or your entire department breaks a record . . . you break your record, and give them the pieces. Go down to your local thrift shop or Salvation Army store and pick up a few old 33-RPM albums. Artists and songs are unimportant but if you can, pick up some records that really annoyed you. This will make the record-breaking process more fun for you. The day after the performance record has been broken, hold a special announcement time and make a spectacle of breaking these albums by smashing them into pieces in front of the entire department to celebrate their broken record. Then sign each piece and make sure each member of the team gets one. There are still record pieces up in the workstations of my people who broke performance records years ago. Simple, inexpensive and fun, these pieces have become cherished keepsakes.

You can also use record-breaking performances as part of your Wall of Fame. I currently have a large cork board on our Wall of Fame titled Broken Records. I use the very same plastic replicas of 45-RPM records and cut them in half so they appear to be broken. Then I determine what productivity standards I want to highlight. I send out a form to all employees to gather information regarding their highest totals in their categories. And having gathered that information, I see who has the highest total in each area, the person who currently holds the record. I use simple white labels to write the person's name, the category and his 'record performance.' Whenever an employee breaks a record, he notifies his supervisor for authorization. Then we hold a public celebration in our weekly sales meeting to recognize any broken records. The new record holder is awarded the plastic record with a new label indicating the new record performance and his name. He puts it up on the board on our Wall of Fame. Also, I use a different color label whenever a specific label is broken to track how many times it has fallen. This Wall of Fame board is probably my favorite way to recognize those who set new records because it is visible to everyone in the department or company. This inspires everyone to become one of the names on these broken records and they will work harder to get there. And this means more success for you and your employees. Sounds pretty good to me!

## WHEATIES
### . . . box of cereal for any situation where you want to acknowledge a *champion*.

This one I purposely use rarely, to increase its value. I use a permanent marker to write the following personal message on every Wheaties box I give out (of course, I begin by putting their name on it): **"The definition of champion: one who has defeated all opponents and is ranked #1, superior to all others. Thank you for the effort that makes you the best of the best . . . a champion!"** Over the last ten years, this has

been one of the most popular moti-vators I have ever used. Some of my employees who have received this award have cut off the front of the box and framed it while others have saved the box fully intact. The one thing they've all done is proudly dis-play their champion award in their work area—which generates ongo-ing enthusiasm and motivation.

Here is another addition I've made to our Wall of Fame. Walking through the mall one day I was drawn, as always, into a sports card shop. I spotted some miniature cardboard replicas of Wheaties cereal boxes (with a cutout space for your photo on the front) and my mind started working overtime as to how I could use these as a recognition award for Champions. Beside these were other Wheaties replicas that were a bit larger in the form of a greeting card that also had a cutout space on the front that perfectly fits a 3 x 5 photo. My mind went from overtime to total spaz-out. What a stroke of luck! In minutes, the new program came to me as I conveniently stood over these Wheaties items so no one else would even think about buying them. I was stirring up an exciting new motivational pro-gram that I knew would be a great success.

Every month we select a sales champion according to various levels of sales goals, quotas and performance. The champion is announced and recognized at our weekly sales meeting. And then we take his or her picture twice—once for the front of the miniature Wheaties box that the employee gets for his desk area, the second for the Wheaties card that we put up on the Wall of Fame board during our special ceremony. While we're speaking of pictures, it's a good idea to purchase a Polaroid Camera for your area. These come in handy for added recognition. And while Polaroid film may seem to be ridiculously expensive, the convenience of instant pictures outweighs the expense. There is also the perfect white space at the bottom of these pictures for the champion to autograph his photo. This works particularly well for the sales champion frame for each month. Not only is his picture on the front but it's autographed as well. My employees feel so proud when I take their picture and have them sign it before I put it up.

Finally, we schedule the day and time for the spine-tingling championship walk. Everyone forms a line going back from the Sales Champion board. And while the famous Queen song, We Are The Champions, reverberates through the room, the Sales Champion walks through the line of his fellow colleagues getting high-fived and patted on the back. At the end of the line I hand him the Wheaties card with his photo (and an "atta boy" message from me) and he puts it up in the appropriate month. Can you imagine the stimulation of walking down the aisle lined with your colleagues offering their congratulations to you, who defeated all others, the champion! Then we schedule the Breakfast of Champions when I take the winner and his supervisor out to a special breakfast at a location of their choice.

If you're interested in using this exceptional motivational program, here is the name of the card store in Chicago that can set you up with the same Wheaties boxes and cards that made it possible. Be sure to tell Jerome that you got the number from this book and that I told you to call. He'll give you a special price.

J's Sports Card Attic, 7601 S. Cicero Ave, Chicago, IL 60652
Phone 773-585-4204   Fax 773-785-6525

## LION

### . . . small rubber figurine of the lion from The *Wizard of Oz* for the employee who exemplifies *courage*.

Have this one mounted on a small trophy block with an inscription plate that includes the employee's name, the year, and the words 'MOST COURAGEOUS' in large capital letters. Select an employee, for example, who may have experienced excessive struggles that year and made it through. Or someone who overcame his fears of dealing with some aspect of the job and learned to excel. I also use a figurine of the Tin Man for the employee with the 'biggest heart.' I always choose someone who has displayed care for fellow employees throughout the year and shows a willingness to help. I only present these two awards once a year at the annual banquet along with other unique recognition awards. These always make the right people feel appreciated for special reasons outside of their performance. These figurines are easy to find at comic book and sports card stores at a reasonable price.

## RESERVED PARKING SPACE
### . . . for the employee who *drives* the hardest.

This award should only be presented weekly or possibly monthly. The winner won't always be the most productive or the one with the highest level of performance. This is for the person whom you feel works the hardest toward his or her goal. Consider factors such as number of phone calls, hours worked, intensity toward the goal, work ethics, determination, perseverance and other indications of someone who simply drives the hardest. Do some of those factors seem subjective? You're right, they are. This award is based as much on feeling as hard facts.

## SUPERMAN/WONDER WOMAN
### . . . for a performance worthy of these *action heroes*.

Comic book or sports card stores and specialty entertainment stores like Warner Brothers and Disney are your best bets to find Superman and Wonder Woman in various sizes and poses. These awards are a little more expensive so you can rotate them on a weekly or monthly basis or reserve them for the annual presentation. Which employee moves faster than a speeding bullet, able to leap tall buildings in a single bound . . . and so on? Determine the criteria that qualifies a performance worthy of

Superman for the men and Wonder Woman for the women, set up your time frame and reward your true super heroes. To add value and fun to your presentation, Superman's cape and other paraphernalia for both of these heroes can be found wherever Halloween costumes are sold.

## SHARK
### . . . rubber or plastic replica of a great white shark, for the employee who represents *aggressiveness.*

Like the raisin, the shark can be mounted and transferred from winner to winner as a weekly or monthly award or just presented once a year. It's effective either way by association. Is there anything on the face of the earth that's more powerful and aggressive than the great white shark? (If you think of something like maybe a tiger, feel free to use it for variety.) Try to determine who among your employees is aggressive. Look for things like the high-intensity pursuit of productivity goals, or the number of outbound calls per day, or even general work habits—depending upon how aggressively people conduct themselves. Determine the qualifying criteria and then go with it. This award is a favorite and naturally promotes a little aggression among many employees to win it.

## "CAN DO" AWARD
### . . . 12-ounce cans of Mountain Dew for employees who exemplify the *can do* attitude.

While these could be reserved as a special annual award, they can also be given out on a regular basis. I give out a few every week so people can build a collection. The number you give out would depend on the number of people in your department, division or company. Let's face it, attitude is everything. So why not reward positive attitudes in your environment? In our workplace, this award has become so special and the status so important that if I go a short time without handing them out, my people let me know. Boy, do they let me know! I always add a small extra that makes for a big addition. I pick up some gold colored star stickers and before I peel them off the sheet, I take a permanent magic marker and write, "Can Do! Thanks!" and I sign it. This personalizes it from you, their leader.

Recognizing positive attitudes promotes continued productivity from the recipients. And you'll be pleasantly surprised by the improvement in attitudes—and from some unexpected people. There's no excuse for not using this one. Head down to your local grocery, pick up a few 12-packs or cases of Mountain Dew. It's on sale right now at the greatest price ever. How do I know how much it sells for in your area? I don't. It doesn't matter. What I do know is that the 40 cents per can is insignificant compared to the impact and therefore the greatest sales price ever.

## MR. PEANUT
### . . . for the employee who has simply *gone nuts* with his or her sales or performance.

Remember the Planters Peanut guy with the black top hat, black and white spat shoes and a cane? I found him at Spencer Gifts. I use this one as a traveling award. Pick a specific time frame of every two weeks, monthly or every week if you want. Take this guy and get him mounted at the trophy shop with a plate that reads "GONE NUTS." Decide on your criteria and get him making his rounds in your area. If you can't find the Planters guy, you can always use the figurine of a squirrel.

## NAIL
### . . . a large nail mounted on a wooden trophy block for the person who *nails down* the most sales.

This monthly or annual sales award couldn't be simpler. Go to a hardware store and purchase the largest nail they have (you can find them 10 to 12 inches long). Then mount it on a trophy block and you're set to go. Like many of these awards, this one is very inexpensive, easy to assemble and means a lot to the winner. Does it get any better than this?

## E.T.
**. . . a figurine of the famous little alien, awarded to the employee with the most out *of this world* performance.**

Mount E.T. on a trophy block with an inscription plate, decide on a time frame (quarterly or monthly works best for this one), the qualifications for what determines the out of this world performance (highest percentage of quota, most sales, etc.) and present it regularly. Small plastic globes with stands are an alternative to E.T. and work just as well. I pick these up at Wal-Mart for about $3 each and present them monthly or quarterly.

## EVEREADY BUNNY
**. . . for the employee who *keeps on going and going and going.***

Toy and specialty stores sell this familiar little battery bunny that keeps on banging his drum. Present this award for continuous effort and perseverance on a weekly or monthly rotating basis, or present it to the one deserving employee once a year. Either way, once you've mounted it, be sure to get an inscription plate that says this employee "keeps on going and going and going."

## TOOTSIE ROLL
**. . . large Tootsie Roll replica (tube or container that holds small Tootsie Rolls and looks just like one) presented every week to the employee who's *on a roll.***

You can buy these at the dollar store at the mall. I just bought five of them the other day. Dump out the little Tootsie Rolls into a bowl and pass those around at work or leave the bowl out for everyone to enjoy whenever they want. Mount and label this award 'You're on a roll!' and put together your determining factors or qualification criteria. You're set to go. People appreciate this one because it signifies continuous success. You will find some people trying vigorously to stay on a role so they don't have to give it up.

## PILLSBURY DOUGHBOY
### . . . for the employee who *raises the most dough*.

This particular award has been among the most coveted awards in every company I've been with. I have also learned through many of your phone calls that it has also gained equal popularity in departments across the country following my consulting assignments. It's not hard to figure out why. First of all, is there anyone out there who doesn't like the Pillsbury doughboy? What could anyone have against this guy? Let's face it, for years we have all melted a little whenever he giggles and moans after having that puffy little tummy gently pushed in with that famous finger, right? It would probably be considered un-American or inhumane to dislike this commercial icon.

This award is really set aside for sales applications and can be implemented for monthly, quarterly and or annual recognition. It goes to the employee who sells the highest volume of dollars or raises the most dough. You can easily find all kinds of variations of this popular character from refrigerator magnets

to key chains to small stand-up figurines. If any portion of your call activity is sales oriented or revenue-generated, this award is a must in your area and will certainly invite some healthy competition for its ownership.

I have also added this board to our Wall of Fame so everyone can see the people who have set the sales standards for everyone to follow. While the winning employee receives the actual doughboy as recognition (which he usually displays in his work area), we also generate a recognition sheet on the computer that identifies the winner's name, the sales volume, number, and the month and year. Then we list these by month on our big Wall of Fame corkboard with the title, "Raised the Most Dough" For veteran salespeople this could be named Raised the Most Motivation because it often does.

## TOY DRUM
### ... for the employee who *drums up* the most business.

This goes to the person who drums up the highest number of sales or the most business in dollars. The drum skin provides a perfect location for a message of congratulations from you. This award works well on a monthly, quarterly or annual basis and works well in conjunction with the doughboy. If the doughboy goes to the person who raises the most dough, the drum can be presented to the employee who drums up the most sales. Usually the recipients will be two different people but sometimes it could certainly be the same person.

## MOVIE PRODUCERS ACTION BOARD
### ... for your *best producer.*

I can already hear your question, "What is an action board?" An action board is that famous little hand-held board used by movie producers with the movie name, scene number and takes. You remember the guy who stands in front of the camera and says, "Scene 2, take 4, and action!" and he bangs the top piece of wood onto the bottom plate. Years ago these were tough to find but now they're available at Spencer Gifts, Warner Brothers or Disney stores from $4 to $6 apiece.

You can vary your schedule for presenting this as a monthly, quarterly or annual award for your best producer, or rotate it weekly or monthly by changing the name on the front of it. This award has always been popular and motivational because it stands for both action and best producer.

## SPARK PLUG
### . . . for the employee who *sparks* (motivates) the other employees the most.

Go to your friendly neighborhood auto parts store, pick up a dozen sparkplugs and have them mounted on small trophy blocks with small inscription plates that read Spark Plug of the Month (or quarter). This award is most effective when you turn the decision over to your employees and let them vote on the winner. You can approach this in various ways. One way is to invite everyone to vote for one person, and the person receiving the most votes wins. Another option is that you and your management team (if you have one) select three to five final candidates and, using a simple voting ballot, let everyone vote for one of them.

The Spark Plug award offers two incentives. First, it signifies having a positive impact on other people. And second, the recipient is selected by the vote of teammates and colleagues. Like many of these awards, this simple and inexpensive gimmick pays great motivational dividends, both short- and long-term. I also present this as an annual award using a larger plaque with a picture slot for a regular size print and spark plug mounted in each top corner and a large inscription plate for Spark Plug of the Year. The picture of the winning employee goes into the photo slot and it gets mounted on our large Wall of Fame for ongoing display. You'll find that all forms of these awards inspire positive attitudes.

## QUEENS, KINGS AND ACES
### . . . to recognize your employees as
### *Queen/King of Sales* for a day or a week.

While you're at the party supply store getting some of your other motivational trinkets, pick up these gigantic playing cards (by the pack or individually). I'm not talking about the ones that are a teeny bit larger than normal cards. I'm talking about the ones measuring about 18" x 24"— some are bigger. Decide what determines King or Queen for a Day (or week) and rotate these large cards daily or weekly. Always take a magic marker and sign the card with an encouraging message of congratulations. These hang up nicely in any workspace and because they're large they're conspicuous. If you have workstations that are built with standard padded wall dividers, you can display these cards between the padding and the frame on the top, which stands them up above everybody and everything else.

## GUMBY
### . . . presented to the one who
### exemplifies the most *flexible* employee.

While this award does not stand for high productivity, big sales or generated revenue, it has been a fairly popular annual award as it represents the valuable ability to adjust to whatever comes along. Deserving employees include someone who had to adjust to unusual situations personally or professionally or someone who endures change well. Perhaps your programs have changed or someone was asked to switch to a new position or take on additional responsibilities. This stretchy little Gumby can be found at Spencer Gifts or other specialty stores for less than five dollars and mounted at the trophy shop. And he'll bring appreciation and ongoing motivation to the winner. Let's face it, not everyone is flexible. When we find people who are, let's recognize them.

87

Some new ideas for awards literally threw themselves at me one day, when I was in a store at the mall called Lechters. Lechters sells all kinds of picture frames and housewares—not the kind of place I'm drawn to. But that day while accompanying Kath on her errands (as a candidate for the good husband award), I discovered a gold mine of award ideas. I came face to face with that tall rotating pillar of refrigerator magnets and all I saw were new award ideas. To my wife's dismay, I turned into the kid in the candy store. I must have acted like a crazy man spinning this thing around looking frantically from one magnet to the next, ideas exploding in my mind. While I'm sure I did not exemplify adult behavior at that moment, one thing is for sure. I had struck motivational gold. Following are a few of the magnets that have become status symbols in my department as annual awards. Have your trophy shop mount them on small wooden blocks or plaques with a creative inscription plate to identify the award.

**CLOTHES IRON**
**. . . for the manager, team leader or supervisor who irons out the most *wrinkles* (problems) in your department.**

**WEIGHT SCALE**
**. . . for the individual that's a "10" when it comes to work ethics. You can give this out to multiple individuals.**

**TELEPHONE**
**. . . for the individual who *rings up* the most sales or calls. These telephones come in different styles so you can give out two or three different ones to the top performers in this category.**

**CAMERA**
. . . to the model individual who
represents the *picture-perfect* employee.

**JUKEBOX**
. . . for the supervisor, team leader or manager
who keeps his team upbeat, active and
productive, or *Rockin' & Rollin* the best.

**BOOK OF MATCHES**
 . . . for the employee who motivates or *fires up*
everyone else (similar to the spark plug award).

These are some of the gimmicks I have used and there are many
more ideas to come. I still have several magnets that I bought
and put aside that I haven't figured out what to do with yet.
They were all so tempting that I couldn't stop buying them
ahead of figuring out how to use them. In one of my previous
work environments, my sales people actually wrote each of
their sales on special sales boards. I found a magnet of a miniature Monopoly game board, which I awarded to the person who
made the most trips to the sales board—the most boardwalks.
Use your imagination and have fun.

Your people will cherish these awards far more than the
typical generic trophies and ribbons—or even cash. During my
presentations and seminars the most frequently asked question
is "Where do you get this neat stuff?" You don't have to ask any
more. I made it easy for you by including all the answers in this
chapter. And remember that imagination shouldn't stop with
positive recognition awards like all of those we've talked about.

You can also develop creative motivation for those who are
not producing so well. Here are a couple of ideas that I have used
with great success.

**KETCHUP**
**. . . plastic bottles of Ketchup placed above the work-**
**stations of those employees who are behind their**
**quotas or goals and need to play *catch up*.**

**DRAGON**
**. . . a toy dragon for the workstations of those**
**employees who find their sales numbers behind or**
***draggin* for the week or the month.**

These are just a couple of the possibilities that help motivate your people into better performance. Think about it for a
minute. Would you want either of these in your workstation for
long? Of course not. They're embarrassing. And that's exactly
why most people work harder to make sure they don't remain
there for long.  Make sure when using any type of negative
award, that you build humor into the situation. Be especially
careful to avoid any kind of serious humiliation that could be
counterproductive.

In all of my work environments, the overall positive impact
from gag and gimmick awards has been immeasurable. And
because the awards are all unique, they are more popular than
any other awards I've ever developed. More popular means
more valuable and more valuable means more effective. Most
importantly, have fun with these. Your employees will love them.

# 6

# One-on-One Coaching

One-on-one coaching addresses two critical issues that produce employee motivation. First, the technique of one-on-one—giving someone individual attention—always stirs motivation. If you don't think this is true, think back to your childhood. Can you remember having some undivided attention from your mom or dad when they were teaching you something like reading, riding a bicycle, throwing a baseball, or baking cookies? Do you remember how special that time felt? Your parents were dedicating their time just to you. And in addition to all that special attention, you were learning something too.

Well, I'm here to tell you that age makes no difference. In some ways we will always be kids. And those same feel good emotions are inside your employees always waiting for your special attention, waiting to learn something from you. Do you ever give your employees one-on-one time? While you're thinking about that, let's look at the second important issue, coaching. I believe it's so important for managers and supervisors to understand what coaching means and how to do it. Let's look at the dictionary definitions:

**Coach**: *n. A private instructor. — v. To teach, train or act as a coach.*

91

**Manage**: *v. To direct or control the use of; to exert control over. To make submissive. To direct or administer.*

Do you see the difference? Managing and coaching are different activities. Managing your employees means just that, managing or directing them. Coaching means employee development, and here lies its motivational value. For most employees, development and progress bring higher motivation.

Sports teams are a good example. Coaching plays a big role in the success of the individual players and therefore, the success of the overall franchise. Coaches help players develop into better players. The better they get, the better they play, the more money they make, and so on. Is it really so different with your team? I don't think so. Your team also wants a coach who can help them become better players so they can continue to grow in success, status and income. Managing means telling someone to do something and overseeing the results. Coaching means showing someone how to do something and continuing to refine skill sets through attention and teaching. Ask yourself, do your people see you as a manager or coach?

Coaching is a full-time job and you as a leader should think, act and react like a coach at all times. I can suggest some times when one-on-one coaching can and should be a part of your schedule.

### 1. Call Monitoring

Monitoring employee calls for performance evaluation provides one of the perfect times for the old coach to step in. Think about why you are monitoring in the first place. I hope the answer is what it should be, to identify your employees' strengths and weaknesses of script presentation, answers to objections, and general sales skills. And if that's your answer (and it better be), think about the opportunity here for one-on-one coaching. You sit and listen to individual employees and identify specific areas for immediate and ongoing improvement. What comes next? Do you walk right out and talk with the employee about what you heard and discuss the ways that he or she might improve presentation or responses to objections? Do you write your suggestions on forms that you can review with them after you monitor them? Or like too many managers and supervisors, do you delay your post monitor meetings until you can schedule a more convenient time? You can be honest; I've done it, too, so I know what happens. Either the more convenient time never comes or you wait too long and your employee can no longer remember the call(s) you monitored. While your coaching may still be helpful at this later time, the effectiveness will certainly be diminished. Immediate attention is the key. I learned the difference between immediate attention and waiting for a more convenient time—and by difference I mean effectiveness.

Now let's return to our teams and coaches analogy. Can you picture a coach watching his players in action, seeing areas that need improvement but saying to himself, "I'll make sure to get with that guy next week sometime and help him get better at that." When I helped coach my son Danny's football team last year I witnessed the finest display of coaching by Rich Wingo, one of our head coaches. Rich was a collegiate star linebacker for the University of Alabama leading to a very successful NFL career. Every practice I watched in awe as Rich would teach these twelve-year-old boys how to be the very best football players. Notice, I didn't say tell them, I said teach them. Teach means to show and to educate by example, whenever possible. Whenever he spotted a flaw, he would promptly get into position, showing them how to stand and how to position their bodies. And then he'd walk and talk them through whatever exercise needed improving. That's what coaching is all about. I was proud just to be part of that coaching staff.

Because of his past experience, Rich could relate to each situation. He could show and teach the boys everything about situations they would face. Once again, is that so different from your lives as leaders in our telemarketing environments? I don't think so. Because of your past experience you can teach and show your players everything they need to know to be the most successful professionals they can possibly be. Yes, I know that takes time. And maybe you don't know how to find the time. Now hear me. You simply have to make the time. The key phrases here are have to and make. I know what your schedules are like. I've lived every one of them. I appreciate the busy schedule that a supervisor, manager or even a team leader in our industry faces. I am also keenly aware of the goals and objectives that most of you are charged with. Again, you have to make the time for this necessary responsibility of monitoring followed by one-on-one coaching. One goes with the other, like peanut butter and jelly, chocolate and milk, Simon and Garfunkel, and so on. Individually, they're good; together they're powerful.

You may be asking, "How long of a wait after monitoring is too long to wait before coaching?" Post monitor coaching carries the biggest punch when it immediately follows your monitoring session—or at least in the same day—while everything is fresh in everyone's mind. I have also been known to do some real-time coaching during monitoring. I jot down an idea and then run out and show it to the salesperson while he's still talking to the prospect or customer. This has sometimes made the difference in the success of the phone call so I recommend keeping a notepad and marker handy and keeping your wheels loose so you can take off at any time. Coaching after monitoring should take place in a place that ensures privacy. But there's one exception. When you hear a superb presentation, strong answers to objections, a successful close or any successful telephone techniques, go out to your employees and share your excitement and appreciation at their work area. And because we've been sharing so many ideas in this book, you know exactly what I'm going to say next. You do this for double stimulation. First, you're motivating the employee you're praising. And second, everyone who hears these public strokes will want to hear some of their own. Don't be surprised if you're visiting other areas over the next few days. While it is healthy and powerful to praise people in public, I am equally strong about my belief in the need for privacy when discussing concerns or areas for improvement.

Don't misunderstand the difference between concerns and encouragement. Of course I believe in encouragement in front of others. Just make sure that it's really encouragement and that you deliver it as praise. One-on-one coaching is not limited to encouragement or a high-five. It can also include the discipline of identifying areas for improvement. This process is what makes them develop, and makes them better salespeople. And whenever the need arises be sure to talk about it in private. Suggestions that are made in private are less intimidating to the employees and will therefore be better received. In fact, I recommend sitting with the employee during the coaching sessions, not on the other side of the desk. This makes the process more personal and will often diminish any anxiety the employee may feel about the coaching session. I firmly believe that embarrassment and public humiliation are not effective or professional ways to improve someone's skills. The only thing this method increases is your turnover percentage.

To summarize, monitoring is a perfect opportunity for you as a leader to provide one-on-one coaching time with your employees, time that you can't afford not to take. Public strokes are appropriate and recommended for praiseworthy efforts, but concerns should be dealt with in private. If you invest some time in coaching you will actually see a return of more time. Your employees will need less maintenance, have more success and stay longer on the job. If this sounds like inside information again, it is, so invest your time now and on an ongoing basis.

## 2. Monthly/Quarterly Employee Coaching Sessions

When is the last time you scheduled a brief session with your employees to discuss their progress and your thoughts about areas of improvement? I'm serious, when was the last time? Unfortunately, the answer is probably "When I do their annual review." Have you ever heard that irritating buzzer that sounds on a game show for the wrong answer? Well, it just went off. Talking to your employees once a year about their performance (because you have to) does not qualify as employee development or motivation. While monthly sessions may not be feasible if you have too many employees, quarterly sessions are certainly workable. And since you are their leader, these meetings belong in your schedule. We're not talking about long hours here, but short 15- to 20-minute sessions. Schedule these times every quarter to make sure you and your employees block off the necessary time. These brief sessions become important to the employees and therefore, motivational. It's a fact that most people want to succeed at their jobs. Therefore, these scheduled sessions make your employees feel they are getting the leadership attention and direction they need to meet their responsibilities.

As the basis of discussion, use their last performance evaluation or the goals that you have mutually agreed upon for that person. This gives you a solid foundation for one-on-one coaching. Briefly talk about what the goals are, where he stands in regards to those goals, and your observations and ideas on how he can be the very best at what he does. Always save a few minutes for him to discuss the training resources he feels would best help him to achieve greater success. And to make sure your feedback is well received, be sure to lace your constructive criticism with some positive comments. As we discussed earlier, it's not just what you say but how you say it that shapes the way your employee hears the information. Don't misunderstand. I am not suggesting that you pacify your employees with undeserved adulation in some sentimental tone. But I promise you that presenting solid developmental suggestions in a healthy, constructive way will be far more productive than blasting someone for his weakness. This is the art of coaching.

In addition, these sessions will prevent any possible shock at the annual review, and that's exactly what they should do. How often did your annual review make you wish that your boss had communicated his concerns earlier in the year so you could have been working on improvement? In my opinion, you are cheating your employees if you don't schedule these coaching sessions each quarter. And you are also cheating yourself, your division and your company. When you include this practice in your motivational game plan you will have a more productive and successful team. Do you see the equation here? It's like a snowball rolling downhill gathering more snow and force as it rolls. You start the ball rolling by scheduling the sessions in advance, which sends a clear message to your employees that you care about their development. The very act of scheduling gives them instant motivation. There is also a natural tendency for the employee to push harder in the time approaching the session. After all, nobody wants to discuss his progress when his recent past is looking anything but good. In other words, the momentum has started.

During the actual session, sit with the employee and discuss his goals and his progress toward these goals. You offer constructive ideas to further his performance while giving recognition of his strengths wherever your praise is deserved. Now the employee can move to improve in the areas you've mentioned, and he will likely show improvement in his attitude and skill sets as well. With this system, there will be few or no surprises at the annual review, making an otherwise tense meeting a more positive review. And the icing on the cake is that the better the annual review the better the chance for a higher merit increase for the employee. And guess whom the employee credits in part for the raise? That's right, you. While they're proud of their own accomplishments throughout the year, they will also be appreciating your dedication to their development through these brief quarterly coaching sessions—and rightfully so.

You can play devil's advocate and try to uncover some kind of downer to this process but I'm going to save you some time and energy. There isn't one. Take advantage of this wonderful opportunity to motivate and develop your employees in one stroke. If you're currently doing this, congratulations! Keep it going strong. If you're not holding these sessions, get out your calendar now and figure out where they fit. Once you've begun, you'll never understand how you did without them.

These two valuable exercises in one-on-one coaching produce a third motivational opportunity, something I refer to as employee-driven sessions. When your employees sense your dedication to their development they grow more comfortable and confident in asking you for additional coaching throughout the year. I have found that the positive impact of these requested sessions is equal to and in some cases surpasses the scheduled sessions. Why? Because the employees have come to you. And as busy as (they know) you are, you took the time when they needed you. And that's the key, recognizing that nothing could be more important than the development of your people. If this sounds familiar, it's because this is like being parents. When my children ask for my help and I put my busy world on pause to pay attention, listen and help however I can, it always means more than when I approach them. I know what you're thinking. "Sometimes, Dave, I'm just so busy, maybe too busy." I understand so busy but not too busy. When my people say to me, "Do you have a minute?" I often respond the same way, "Having one and taking one are two different things. Of course,

I'll take a minute, what's on your mind?" What I said is while I don't have one, I'll take one because you're that important." It's no wonder that this response motivates them. And the busier you are, the more it will mean to them to have you take that time when they ask.

As we said in the beginning of this chapter, one-on-one coaching may feel like a full-time job. But as a leader, you are unquestionably responsible for the productivity and performance of your people. This is just another easy and effective way of motivating your people to be the best they can be.

# 7

# Executive Recognition

I n times of war, the term secret weapon refers to a powerful hidden arsenal that is used only on occasion but produces a big bang. Would you agree that you and I are in battle everyday at work? I'm glad we got that straight. We are at
war against turnover, the evils of gossip and negative people,
and the obstacles to reaching goals and quotas. We are always
trying to recruit the right people and find the time to train. Business provides the everyday challenge of developing and maintaining an environment where our employees are motivated. It
is an endless battle.

Since the war will probably never be over, we as leaders continue to battle as hard as we can with every viable weapon we
can get our hands on. The subject of this chapter, executive
recognition, would definitely be classified as a secret weapon in
our battle of employee motivation. And like any secret weapon,
timing is the key element. If we use it with good strategy and
only on rare occasions, we can produce potent results. If we use
it too often, the effect goes way down. Remember the previous
chapter on recognition and attention? It's a fact that employees become motivated by recognition for a job well done. It is
also true that the impact gives even better mileage when the
recognition comes from a higher level executive than from the
immediate supervisor or manager.

Let's slow down and examine this more closely before your ego gets in the way. I'm referring to the old "they must want the executive's approval more than mine" syndrome. And maybe that hurts a little. Well, don't let it because (1) this is not personal, and (2) it isn't true anyway—at least not in most cases or not for long. You are a more active leader in your employees' professional lives. You live with them from day to day, while this executive may only have fleeting moments with any of them, if any at all. That's precisely why you can use this form of non-monetary motivation with such great success if you don't get caught in jealousy. Taken from another angle, think back to your childhood. Did you have that one special grandparent whose approval meant the world to you? While your mom and dad may have recognized you many times for the same achievement, somehow it was extra special coming from grandma or grandpa. Or take the example of sports. While you may have been recognized many times for your achievements by an assistant or specialty coach, wasn't the praise a little more special coming from the head coach?

Last year I helped coach my son's football team. One of our head coaches, who was also in charge of the offense, asked me to be his assistant offensive coordinator. I have the same principles on the football field as in business or at home when it comes to delivering encouragement and recognition. Working mostly with the offensive backfield of Jake Wingo, Blake Harper and Trey Oswalt, I often got a chance to verbally recognize their visible achievements both in practice and during games. "Jake, what a move, great touchdown run!" or "Blake, that touchdown pass was a perfect throw, great job!" or "Trey, way to hit the hole quick and hard, great touchdown run!" I know they appreciate my enthusiasm and my recognition of their achievements but you can easily tell that the same statement means a little more when it comes from Coach Fred or Coach Rich, the big guys, because it's coming from the top, the head coaches. And it should; this is normal. Should I feel slighted? Of course not. In fact I find myself even happier and prouder of them when the two head coaches verbally applaud them.

Go back to school for a minute and remember a time when you received special recognition from the principle for something—maybe your grades, your athletic achievements, or a role in a play. Even though you were probably recognized by your teacher, coach or drama leader, didn't it mean just a little more coming from the principle, the big seat? Of course it did. That's only natural, and that's my point. If you are a parent, turn it around now. Haven't there been times when recognition from the grandparents seems to mean more to your kids than your praises do? And maybe you catch yourself thinking, "Wait a minute, you weren't that excited when I congratulated you." Boy, have I had those times. You have to step back and get a grip. You're the parent, the norm, the everyday leader, and the one they hear it from all the time. Does that diminish the value of your praise? Absolutely not! My kids love it when Kathy and I take them out for ice cream. But it's always extra special when the grandparents take them. It's different; it's mom and dad's mom and dad. In reality, aren't you happy for your kids when they receive special attention from someone other than you? I sure am. And this applies to your employees. Don't let your ego mislead you. Furthermore, you should be the one to ensure that executive recognition takes place. Many executives are unaware of the effect of their attention on their employees. And they will depend on your ideas for the right timing as well as how to do it. You have to initiate this gesture. And you have to make it as easy as possible for the executives to get involved. You should document whatever is relevant and prepare it for the executive. If it's a performance-based issue, write down the totals for the executive so he has the particulars for making the recognition accurate and personal. If your employee met an important project deadline, jot down the details so the executive can talk about the time frames and their significance. If someone broke a previous productivity record, note the previous record and the new total so the executive can speak about both when congratulating him. Remember that this creates twice the stimulation because when the executive recognizes your employee, the employee will realize that you took the initiative to share his success with the top.

Now let's consider three ways in which executives can recognize the employees—verbal recognition, written recognition and family ties.

## VERBAL RECOGNITION

Remember our discussion about verbal recognition in chapter two, about how easy this is and how much it means to the employee? The windows of opportunity for this recognition remain the same. It can take place over the phone, on voice mail, during morning announcements (if you have them), in meetings, at social gatherings, at company parties and in person.

## 1. Phone Calls

The telephone is the world's most powerful communication tool, especially in our business. Let's use it. Have the executive make a quick phone call to your deserving employee any time during the course of a workday to thank him for his special job performance level. Think about the shock and surprise. Can you see his face? He's doing his routine daily tasks and suddenly he gets a call from the top? The top brass is calling to thank him for his contribution? Just to be safe, you might want to keep some smelling salts in your first-aid cabinet. Maybe we're exaggerating a little here but not about the power of this telephone call. It's incredible. Not only will this recognition ignite the employee but it will be far too big for him to keep to himself. Before long, the buzz will be out. This kind of news is too good not to share. Almost no one could sit on a secret like this. And

103

as he proudly spreads the news, he is spreading motivation everywhere. The other employees will also want a call like this, so they will push harder than ever to make it happen for them. Do you see what I mean? A simple phone call produces endless reverberation. How much time does it take? A minute or two. The positive repercussions? Immeasurable.

## 2. Voice Mail

Voice mail provides another means for executive recognition. As we discussed in Chapter 2, voice mail messages usually communicate demands, project deadlines and other business emergencies. But then right in middle of all that dry business— WHAM! They get hit with an exciting message from the top congratulating them on a great job. I wonder how many times a message can be listened to before it wears itself right off the tape? You will probably find out because I guarantee they'll play these messages MANY times over. And they'll want to keep this message in voice mail archives as long as possible so they can listen to it whenever they like and share it with others.

Be sure to encourage the executives to copy your voice mailbox on any of these motivational messages they leave for your employees. Then you can stimulate the employee all over again when you tell him that you also received a copy of the message. Voice mail provides the perfect means for executive recognition. It requires such a small investment of time and effort and it yields a truckload of motivation in return. And that kind of motivation will always boost performance, productivity, loyalty and dedication, as well as a reduction in turnover. Sound like a good deal to you? If not, call your doctor for an immediate appointment. You've got a major chemical imbalance.

## 3. Personal Visits

While voice mail and phone calls are perfect tools for employee recognition, personal visits will turn up the motivational

104

juices even higher. Again, we're not talking about executives having to put aside hours of time that they don't have. This gesture requires very little time but packs a big punch. If you're a parent, you've read the books that say it's not the quantity but the quality of time you spend with your children that makes the difference. This is no different. Put yourself in the employee's shoes and picture the next scene. It's a normal day in your office, business as usual, and suddenly it happens. The door opens and in walks the big boss, the head honcho, the proverbial big cheese. And in front of everyone the executive walks straight toward you. This is when you start feeling the shaky knees, the dry throat and general panic. Then you imagine embarrassing scenarios like "Is my tie crooked?" or "Do I have poppy seeds stuck in my teeth?" or worse, "I wonder if something is hanging out of my nose!" And then as the executive closes in on you, you fear the typical "Oh no, what did I do wrong?" And then there he is, standing in front of you while your colleagues watch and listen. The executive congratulates you—he shakes your hand, praises you and recognizes you for your achievements.

During this encounter you may be in a daze oblivious to the outside world; but then it hits you. You know what's going on and it feels great. "Here is one of the brass telling me what a great job I'm doing." This hits the old ego with some velocity doesn't it? And just when you think it can't get any better, you realize that your colleagues are watching. That's what makes this form of recognition so doubly effective. While the executive is sending you off to Cloud 9, your colleagues are wishing the same thing would happen to them. We talked about this earlier. It's only natural. You're motivated to keep working hard and now your co-workers will also be turning up the juice. Get the picture?

Okay, now you can step back into your own shoes again. Another approach is to schedule the executive for a morning or afternoon visit, get everyone off the phone and have the executive recognize the deserving employees in front of everyone. Pre-shift announcement times provide a good opportunity for this. I have done this for many years and it gets the work shift off to such a positive start. While I realize that these visits may not be possible in some firms and geographically impractical in others, I am also sure of one fact. In the corporations and companies where these meetings are feasible they're not happening very often, if at all.  Why not? It couldn't be due to a time shortage because it doesn't require much time. It can't be that executives don't like employee achievements because I'm sure they do. During consulting assignments, I find that the most common reason this is not happening is also the easiest one to change. Managers and supervisors simply haven't taken the steps to work this out with the necessary executives. Take a little time, folks, and make these executive visits a reality in your environment. The executives will love the results and so will you.

## WRITTEN RECOGNITION

While verbal recognition from an executive offers powerful inspiration to the employee, written recognition has the proverbial one-up. A written document carries one BIG difference that in no way belittles verbal praise. The simple difference is that written praise can be saved. It can—and will—be looked at over and over again. In addition, written recognition will get some serious attention because the employee will often post it in a visible spot in his workstation or at least keep it within reach. And every time he sees it the words of appreciation switch on his motivation. These same forms of written recognition that are effective coming from you are also effective when implemented by executives.

### 1. Letters

We talked about how much the employees appreciate a letter

of congratulations or praise for a job well done and the long-term motivational force that it carries. Well, **getting executives involved** in this process puts the icing on the cake. Let's look back at those three words getting executives involved. This is the key. And this is your job. Once again, you will probably need to initiate this process to make it happen. And I guarantee you will want this to happen because it's one of those everybody wins scenarios. The employees win because they receive letters of recognition and this fosters their positive performance, which drives more income, job security, self-esteem, and so on. You win because the employees know that you shared their success with the power tower and therefore they respect and appreciate you more. This drives them to keep working hard for you, which makes them happier, more loyal and productive. This, in turn, lowers turnover and makes for a healthier more successful department under your leadership and brings all the professional and financial benefits that go along with it. The executive wins because he gains respect and appreciation, driving the employee and you to continue working hard for him, along with all the other benefits that impact you. And the company wins because happy, motivated employees are more productive, more profitable, more loyal and dedicated . . . better employees. How much better can it get? Not much. And the technique couldn't get much easier.

All this positivity gets generated because letters of recognition from executives are status symbols. Employees will show their family members, friends and most importantly, their co-workers. I say most important because this creates the old double stimulation again. As soon as co-workers see a letter like this, most of them will certainly want one of their own and will do whatever it takes to get one—and the cycle begins.

As we've discovered with similar forms of motivation, these letters do not have to be long. Just make sure that the executive mentions the specific achievement by the employee and that the letter is copied to you. Since the employee's letter will indicate that you've been copied, you can once again congratulate the employee on his (her) accomplishment. Once again, you get two hits for the price of one. To really cash in, you can duplicate your copy of the letter and write a nice note to the employee from you highlighting the executive's recognition. Sign the note and personally give it to the employee.

Letters of recognition from executives is without question one of the most powerful non- monetary motivational tools. No motivational toolbox should be without them.

## 2. Company Newsletter

Earlier we discussed how you could recognize your employees if your company has an in-house newsletter. This also presents another fine opportunity for executive recognition. Everyone wants to see his or her name in lights. And who wouldn't love being applauded by a high-level executive in front of the whole company? You can make this happen. Notify the appropriate corporate executives of the news, send them the achievements, help with the preparation if needed, and watch the fun begin. You know the look and the reaction. On the outside the employee is saying, "It was nothing, really, it was nothing," while on the inside he's trying to figure out where he can get more copies of the newsletter without seeming arrogant. As a nice gesture, you might even get a few extra copies and surprise him when the newsletter first comes out.

During my employment with Diebold Inc., I developed the telemarketing division that quickly grew from three full-time people and one call function to twenty full-time employees covering product sales, service contract renewal, lead generation and customer satisfaction. No single person (myself included) was responsible for all of the growth. It was a team effort. So I got my boss (an executive) to submit a story that not only educated everyone about our division but also recognized everyone in the department. The story included a picture of our whole team and generated tremendous stimulation among all of the employees. Let me make two points here. First, this type of recognition does not need to be limited to one person. Second, include a picture whenever possible. My entire team was so excited when the photographers came down to take the picture and even more excited to see the picture when the article came out.

This form of executive recognition is simple because the newsletter is already being published on a regular basis. And the whole purpose of the company newsletter is to report company news. Well, give an executive something to report and then sit back and watch the results. One accomplishment applauded in print will create future newsworthy performances.

## 3. Goal Cards

Another simple form of written recognition from executives is to get them involved from time to time in your goal card program. Remember the employees' goal cards (Chapter 2) that get pinned up on the Wall of Fame board titled Goal Busters? I put a sticker and a congratulation message on each one before I return it to the employee. Then periodically, for special accomplishments, have the appropriate executive also sign with a note before the goal card goes back to the employee. This will generate immediate and ongoing inspiration for the employee.

## FAMILY TIES

This form of executive recognition indirectly affects the employee through the family of the employees. In an earlier chapter on recognition we looked at the value of recognizing an employee in front of family members. This is a similar theme. Let's remember that if someone is doing a great job at work, the chances are good that they have a solid support system at home. Indirectly, a spouse or family can play a major role in the

109

success of your employee. Think about it. How effective can an employee be if his spouse doesn't support what he's doing for a living? On the other hand, see how many similar scenarios you can imagine regarding a less productive employee who lives in a non-supportive household. In light of this probability, I ask one question. Wouldn't it be valuable to recognize the people behind the scenes, the people who support your employees' success? Wouldn't they feel good being noticed?

If you've ever watched football, maybe you've seen a running back score a touchdown. I have thousands of times. And what happens after the touchdown? Everyone focuses on the running back. The players and the fans congratulate him. The media interviews him. All the attention goes to the running back. But how often do we look at the blocks that were made to break the running back free so he could score the touchdown? If you think the way I do, the answer is "not often enough," if at all. How many touchdowns could any running back score without the blocks by his teammates? We all know the answer. Isn't this situation parallel to the work place? I think it is. The people behind the scenes are supporting someone else's success but they rarely get recognized, if ever. Well, here's your big chance to make it different. Here's your chance to help your company get away from the cookie cutter mold, to be different and special. Instead of always giving the 'high five' to the running back, let's every now and then give thanks to the teammates who helped make possible the run, the score, and the visible achievement. Following are three opportunities for executive recognition that shows appreciation for the family's contribution to the employee's success.

## 1. Flowers

Every now and then, try sending flowers from an executive to the wife of an employee who deserves recognition. Be sure to have the executive sign one of those little cards that goes with the flowers. He should thank the wife for her husband's good work, with something simple like, "Your husband did a great job on our last project. Thank you for your support," followed by his signature. As Gomer Pyle used to say, "Surprise, surprise, surprise!" You can bet this will be a surprise and a well received one. What woman does not like to get flowers?

Now imagine what happens when your employee gets home from work that day. He gets surprised by a happy and surprised wife. And the stimulation has just begun. First, the wife is now more motivated to support a few late hours of work or business phone calls. And what about your employee? He's now more motivated knowing that the executive not only appreciated his work but also acknowledged him to his family by thanking his wife with flowers for her support. Quick, grab onto something and hold on tight, we're about to experience one of those "9. 7" motivational earthquakes we went through earlier in the book. It doesn't get much better than this or much easier. Do you think it's worth the $30 for the flowers and the two minutes it took to write the note? I think you've just made a pretty good investment—no, a very good investment. And I don't think so. I know so.

## 2. Letter

There are only two differences between the letter and the flowers. First, the appreciation arrives in the mailbox instead of being delivered at the front door. And second, the letter is a little more versatile than flowers because it works equally well for men and women. While I certainly can't speak for everyone, flowers are generally not such a special surprise for the man of the house (thanking him for the job his wife does it work). I just don't know too many men who would appreciate a dozen roses. However, when the roles are reversed, you could send a pair of tickets to a local sporting event or greens fees to a local golf course or something more appropriate to the man's interests.

You have to determine the possibilities.

The letter offers a little more flexibility since written acknowledgement is equally appreciated by both genders. And if you know that your employee has children, be sure to address it to the family of the employee. This way the kids are included and they get to be proud of mom or dad too. The level of surprise is equal to the flowers. And the motivation it generates is just as strong. Picture this scene: You're the spouse going through the mail as usual, and —hold it, go back, what's this? An envelope from your spouse's workplace arriving for me? What do they want with me? Then he (she) opens it and the motivation is underway. And remember we're not talking about a dissertation here. A few brief paragraphs are fine. In case you have to write this letter yourself (as I've had to do on occasion), here is an example of how simple this letter can be:

---

Dear (Name),

Thank you, (Name)! Your (husband/wife) is doing such a great job here at (company name) that I wanted to let you know how much we appreciate (him/her) . . . and you. I'm sure that (he/she) would not have been able to reach 113% of (his/her) monthly quota without your love and support. Again, thank you. Keep up the great teamwork!

Sincerely,

---

This letter is just an example. You can modify this to suit your taste, but remember that it doesn't have to be long. This shouldn't be a time-consuming or a time- robbing exercise. And please don't even think about using a form letter. This is one of those occasions where form letters will not be worth the time you save by having them on standby. The entire purpose of this letter is to individually touch the spouse or family support system of the employee who is performing so well for your company. It would be self-defeating to use some standard letter that generically thanks them with pre-printed sentences that could apply to many other employees. This is not a good idea. In fact, it's a horrible idea so don't do it. Take the time on these rare and special occasions to make this brief letter special. Make it personal and specific regarding the achievements, the appreciation and the recognition.

As we discussed earlier, these letters will get many repeat readings. And every time the employee sees it he'll feel motivated all over again. Every time the spouse or family sees it they'll feel appreciation. And all of this appreciation and motivation gets escalated every time they show the letter to someone else—and they will show it to others. They can't help themselves. The spouse or employee will show the letter to others out of pride. And that's the very nerve we wanted to touch in the first place, along with the initial appreciation to and for the spouse. Pride. According to Webster, pride is defined as proper respect for oneself, a sense of one's own dignity or worth, self-respect. Delight or satisfaction in one's own or one another's achievements. Not only is the employee proud of himself (herself) and feel a sense of worth, but the spouse is proud of his partner and the kids are proud of their parent. And it's all because of this simple letter.

These letters may even become hanging stimulation just as the letters we talked about earlier in Chapter 2. While those letters usually get displayed in the work area of the employee, I have heard many times that these letters get pinned up on the family bulletin board in the kitchen. This makes it very visible very often, and we just discussed the power of this kind of letter that gets looked at regularly.

There's really no magic regarding the timing of these letters but the same basics hold true for all executive recognition. We only use it in rare cases for special accomplishments such as a new sales record, winning a contest, meeting an important project deadline or any other situation that you feel deserves this distinguished recognition.

### 3. Phone Call

You've probably already figured out what this phone call is and how it works but let's go over it anyway. Instead of sending mail or flowers to the spouse or family of the deserving employee, simply pick up the phone. And if you don't believe in the power of the telephone, you're working in the wrong industry! What a great feeling to be answering the phone, expecting something ordinary like a call for the kids, only to be surprised or shocked to hear an executive from his (her) spouse's company telling him how much he is appreciated. These calls draw a similar response as those contest-winning phone calls where the recipient is in disbelief and repeatedly questions the caller and his motives ("No, come on, who is this really?").

Again, the message doesn't have to be long but it must be sincere. If you're going to put aside the few minutes that it takes to do this, don't be in a rush to get off the phone. If you're in a rush, you're going to sound like you're in a rush. If you sound like you're in a rush, you'll dilute the power of the message and miss the value of this fine opportunity. If the recipient senses that you are just rushing through the call, he will believe that there is something more important waiting for you as soon as you can get rid of him. And that's not a good feeling for anyone to have. Make him feel that there is nothing more important than this phone call. And then the recipient's inspiration will be uncontainable. Be sure to discuss the achievement as well as the issue of positive support and appreciation for everyone at the house. Believe it or not, about one to two minutes should

114

be enough to cover everything and then the same long-term motivation will kick in. The spouse hears all about the call, feels tremendous about his job and the executive and then he tells others. And most important, the recipient of the call is most appreciative, which will result in long-term support, probably stronger than ever.

The phone call will probably not maintain the motivation as long as the flowers or letter because it ends quickly with nothing tangible to see, touch or feel. But that's not to say that it won't be equally effective. Employees and their families appreciate all of these gestures and treasure the sense of appreciation they express. In fact, any one of these three ideas will be effective whenever you use it. And part of this effectiveness is the ongoing stimulation that generates ongoing motivation. Do you honestly think that the recipient of any one of these forms of thanks and recognition will keep it to themselves? Not a chance. And that's the beauty of it. They will tell their friends at church, at the grocery store, at school when they're picking up the kids, and everywhere else. How can I be so sure? Because you would too, and so would I. Why? Because it's rare, it's unusual, its special and everyone will want to share it. The good word is out about you, the executives involved and the company, and word of mouth is the strongest form of communication. Very simply put, this is another one of those win/win/win situations.

If you are a company executive, are you involved enough in the success of your employees? If you are, great! If not, now is the time to get involved. If you're a manager or supervisor, it's also your mission to make sure that you get executives involved in the recognition of your employees' achievements. It's easy to organize and the return on your investment will be enormous.

# 8

# Career Path

D o your people know where they're going after this job? Do they know if there are progressive opportunities for them in your department or company? These questions need to be answered and those answers need to be clearly communicated to your employees. Remember that perception is reality. If your employees believe there is no chance for advancement and no opportunity to grow in responsibility and income, why will they want to stay? Would you? Think about your current position and whether there is any room for you to grow. If there is, doesn't that help motivate you to do the best job you can to land a promotion? If your job has no growth potential, isn't it somewhat de-motivating to know that no matter what you do, how hard you work, what you achieve or how many hours you put in, there is no opportunity for advancement? I mean zero, the big goose egg.

A no-growth position is counterproductive for most people. And we all know where this goes. You suddenly become interested in the Sunday classified ads and this becomes a deeper distraction. While I'm sure there are some people who do not want promotions, the majority of people everywhere want a career path that includes position and financial growth. And since we're always taught to manage the masses, let's deal with the fact that most of our people are motivated just knowing there is opportunity beyond what they are doing now. So I ask you again, are there growth opportunities for your employees? If you answered yes, that's great. Now think about these two critical questions. First, are the advancement opportunities attainable? If not, you're spinning your wheels. If they are reachable, that's good. That's how it should be. Then we can move on to the second and more important question, do your employees know what these opportunities are? If you answered yes, you're in fairly good shape and you can get away with skimming this chapter for new ideas. If you answered no, or "I'm too busy to notice," this chapter requires your undivided attention.

The following issue is a sometimes forgotten ingredient in the motivational mix. Do you promote from within? I hope you can answer yes. Although specific circumstances sometimes require you to look for talent outside your company you should always consider internal personnel first.

While you may not be aware of this, whenever you recruit from outside your division or company before looking within your department, you send a clear message to your own employees that says "lack of confidence." In the ongoing effort to motivate your employees, this practice is counterproductive. Although there are times when you are legitimately forced to fill a position from outside, too many managers buy into the new blood theory as in, "We need new blood in here." Where does this idea come from? I'm not trying to insult your intelligence here, but doesn't it make more sense to promote someone who already knows the company infrastructure, who is familiar with your product, who knows the personnel, understands and supports company missions as well as management philosophies and can hit the ground running? If you agree with me, why aren't you thinking about that first? I bet I know. You don't think you have anyone capable of handling the job. If I had a quarter for every time I've heard this, I could retire.

This is the time to look in the old mirror for a much needed reality check. Get in front of a mirror right now; I'll wait. By the way, when you get in front of it, you will see plenty of my marks; I've been there many times before. Okay, ready? Now, if you have to say, "I don't have anyone capable of doing the job," my question is, "Why not?" The answer is the simple but painful truth that your employees must not be developed enough to qualify for the promotion and that's why you're looking in the mirror. It's our job as leaders to prepare our employees for growth. It hurts me even to say that because I've been there and faced it before. I've been guilty of falling short in one of management's most critical responsibilities, developing people for future growth. Okay, now give me a few seconds to brace myself for your attack of reasons that usually start with "if" or "but." Okay, I'm ready, now go ahead. I can hear it now, "Dave, if I only had more time . . . " "But Dave, I really do try . . . " "If my employees were more like me and worked harder..." "I guess I could do more but they should know how to prepare themselves better." We could go on like this all day, right? I know you've got a lot more of these excuses because I used to say the same things. That's right, used to. Now whenever I have thoughts that begin with if or but, I remind myself of the famous words of Don Meredith, a former Dallas Cowboys quarterback and colorful football commentator. After Howard Cosell made three or four defensive arguments about a team's lack of success using if and but, Don calmly replied, "Howard, if ifs and buts were candy and nuts we'd all have a Merry Christmas! There was silence, dead quiet. Can you imagine Howard Cosell speechless? Don's statement is so true. We can't live on ifs and buts.

First, you must figure out who is interested in future growth because as we discovered, a small percentage of your people are not. Then you must identify the developmental needs and desires of these growth-oriented employees and then, most importantly, act on them. Now that you've come this far, don't let yourself get caught up in the following two excuses that all too often stop managers here.

**Excuse # 1:** "We only have a small department, I can't set up a career path."

**Excuse # 2:** "I can't get the budget dollars to promote anyone or begin to set up a career path."

Does this sound familiar? Now let's shoot holes in both of these theories one at a time. First, if you have four or more employees, you can set this up. Why can't one of your four develop into a team leader? Sports teams have player coaches. It's no different. And shouldn't you have a team leader? What happens when you're in meetings? Out of the office? On vacation? Enough said. While motivating these player coaches you are also stimulating the remaining staff by showing them that there is opportunity for growth.

While the size of your department is a tougher target to shoot holes in, "no budget dollars" is not an excuse. In fact, remember those water-cooled Thompson machine guns that the FBI and gangsters used in the old TV series The Untouchables? Well, picture me with one of those right now because I'm about to use it to shoot some serious holes in this feeble excuse. First of all, who said budget dollars are necessary? Not me. Did you? Did you forget what this book is all about? Motivating without money. While an increase in pay may be feasible down the road it is certainly not a requirement to start building a career path in your environment. Later in the book there is a complete chapter on motivation through additional responsibility, but for now let's look at how it relates to a successful career path and the stimulation that it generates. One of my former situations is a perfect, real life example. All of my sales managers were also on the phone, many with the highest quotas in the company. I had about 42 account executives including this management team of six. They had to work so hard every week to meet their sales goals that they had little time to answer questions, monitor calls, or take care of the people under them. Knowing this and realizing the potential for disaster, I created and fine-tuned a plan that would eventually be authorized for implementation. This plan included smaller teams headed up by team leaders. My thought process here was simple. While I was creating a subordinate level of management to intercept some of the day-to-day headaches of questions, complaints and other time-robbers from my overwhelmed managers, I was also developing a more visible career path for sales people. Think about it; if you're a sales person truly looking for a future management position and suddenly a role appears that's an immediate stepping stone to your goal, wouldn't you be pumped? Of course you would. This is natural. The chance to be a leader is suddenly closer and more feasible, and this makes the work environment more stimulating.

Ten people were carefully selected for this new position to lead teams of only two to three people. I knew in advance I didn't have any budget dollars for pay raises and so did the ten new team leaders because I told them as a group after selections were made. They knew right up front that the only thing they would gain right away in their new role was more responsibility and that it was a temporary pilot program to see if it would prove to be positive. But along with the status of leadership, the boost in self-esteem and the challenge of proving this to be valuable enough for a permanent change was more than enough initial stimulation for an enthusiastic start. After five successful months under this new structure, I was able to put proposals in place for additional capital for my team leaders with solid justification behind it. Isn't it easier sometimes to get what you need after you prove its success? I'll even go one step further. Don't you think these team leaders are working even harder to prove the solidity of the program than they might have if everything had been handed over in the beginning? I think so. In fact, I know so. Simple inexpensive differences will also help make these positions a success while pay increases are not yet in the

picture. I orchestrated a product trade with a local sign company for new Team Leader nameplates that were a different
color than those of the sales staff. Even if you're not in position
for a trade, these nameplates are inexpensive and because of
the stimulation they offer, they should be considered an investment rather than a cost. I also held a weekly meeting with them
as a team with hamburgers and fries or pizzas brought in, and
we discussed each week's productivity as well as the upcoming
strategies for the next week. A small investment for a huge
return. This makes them feel a grade higher, a step above . . .
just plain special. And again, while they are stimulated by just
having the chance to become team leaders, I also indirectly
motivated the other sales people because they can now see and
believe in their own growth opportunities.

Most of your employees want to know what lies ahead and
what their chance is for advancement. Don't you? Well, where
do you think you're going if you can't develop anyone to some-
day replace you? In the 1960s vernacular, "This is Nowheres-
ville, man." Unless you provide a career path and help others
grow, you also have no chance to grow. Always remember that
a career path grooms career-minded professionals. Isn't that the
type of person you want?

# 9

# A Good Work Environment

In the introductory chapter we talked about the felony that many telesales managers and supervisors are committing everyday, what I call *motivational murder*. One of the reasons that some of our own are headed for *hard time* is that they are overlooking one of the most important non-monetary motivating factors. They do not believe in the value of a good work environment. Industry studies show how inaccurate our beliefs and theories can sometimes be. In a study on telesales environments, employers were asked to rank what factors motivated their people and then the employees were asked to rank the same factors. Employers felt that out of ten motivating factors, working conditions was near the bottom in terms of their employees' priorities. And guess what the employees said? They rated working conditions near the top almost every time. Well, are you ready to turn yourself in and confess or will we have to issue a warrant for your arrest? Maybe some of you aren't guilty but many of you are. In fact I'll bet some of you were about to blow off this chapter because you didn't feel that environment was an important subject. Well I'm glad you didn't and I hope by the time you finish this chapter you'll be glad too.

The fact that your employees spend more waking hours at work than anywhere else is probably why good working conditions are so important and therefore motivational to them. Before we discuss the specifics, let's once again get into our time capsules and revisit the past. Have you ever worked in a place where the work environment didn't feel very good? Boy I have. If you have too, then let's revisit those days together for a reality check. While company names are certainly not important here, conditions are. Have you ever worked in an environment where the workstations were so close together that you barely had elbow space? Or the furniture was old and worn out? Or the walls were all roughed up without any pictures or posters? Maybe the temperature was never right, either too cold or too warm? If any or all of these sound familiar, think about how you felt about your workplace. The one word that comes to my mind is *embarrassed.* What an unhappy feeling to be embarrassed about the environment you work in. How motivational is that? I used to make up excuses to stop people from coming to my workplace to pick me up or to have a meeting or even to visit me. It was terrible. Perhaps you are working in an environment now that includes some or all of the negative factors we just described. If that's the case, don't worry because the rest of this chapter will offer you some hope. If you happen to be lucky enough to work in first-class conditions, you still may find a few reminders or ideas worth looking at. And if, like most people, your conditions are somewhere in between, there will definitely be some valuable information in the next few pages. Just remember as you are reading that good working conditions are extremely important to your people and therefore a motivational factor. If you read something that you feel will be helpful to your environment, be open enough and flexible enough to initiate some changes

## WORKSPACE

Well, let's get right down to it. Are your folks elbow-to-elbow in the proverbial sardine can workspaces or do they have the room they need to be positive, productive employees? While I'm not suggesting that their workspace has to include a visitor's area and meeting room, they do need a reasonable amount of space to be comfortable. More comfortable will mean more positive and more positive will definitely mean more productive.

Physical comfort is only one-half of the workspace equation. Mental comfort is the other half. One of the keys to success in our industry is organizational skills. Salespeople need to have everything at their fingertips to make solid presentations, answer objections and speak intelligently about products and services. Do your telephone professionals have adequate room for all of their essential materials? Have you ever received a telemarketing call from someone who sounded disorganized? I sure have. This person is not hard to identify and will not be inspirational. You can usually hear the rustling of paper in the background as he struggles to find materials or prices to answer your questions. Is that the perception you want your customers or prospects to have when your people call them? I don't think so. Inadequate space for proper organization can be frustrating and therefore counterproductive. On the flip side, adequate workspace that gives the employee room to move as well as the neutral comfort zone to be organized and better prepared to succeed will definitely be a positive motivator for your people. Check industry magazines and journals for some of the latest statistics and ideas about workspace size, dimensions, and practical needs.

**FURNITURE**

What kind of desks do your employees use? What condition are they in? Are the chairs comfortable? Do they roll back well or do they sit unevenly with a roller missing? What about file space? Do they have enough? Do the drawers work properly? Is *any of this really that important?* Are you serious? As they used to say on Laugh In, "You bet your sweet bippy it is!" These items are all important unless you're not concerned that your uncomfortable, unhappy, semi-productive employees may soon be adding percentage points to your annual turnover.

First let's talk chair. How important is it? Well, let's add two plus two and come up with four. We expect our employees to sit in their chairs most of their working day and be happy, productive people. I guess it would stand to reason that we should provide comfortable chairs for them, huh? Hang on, I know that chairs are expensive. This may sound like a cost but we're talking about an investment. On my consulting assignments, I have seen a noticeable improvement in productivity levels and I've seen the change right before my very eyes. In one company I worked for we changed our old, roughed-up chairs to new chairs for all of our account executives and we saw an immediate increase in performance. Coincidental? Not a chance. For many people who work on their feet all day, shoes are like their chairs. Comfortable shoes are always a top priority because they have to stand in them all day. Do you honestly believe that a person who is wearing uncomfortable shoes all day will be as productive as if they're wearing comfortable shoes? Highly unlikely. Well, in our business our chairs are our shoes. The only difference is that we as the employers are responsible for this comfort zone.

If you've ever had to spend your days in an uncomfortable chair you know what I'm talking about. When chairs are uncomfortable, people simply don't sit in them as much as they should. When they're not in their chairs, they're not making calls. When they're not making calls, they're not productive. When they're not productive . . . how far do you want me to take this? Now let's refer to the original question, how important is a comfortable chair? I think we just established the answer. Let's move on to the desk.

We've already covered the importance of the size of the desk to meet the organizational needs. While we're not talking about some monstrous cherry wood desk and credenza, the desk size should allow for the storage of necessary supplies, product information, some or all files, and have enough space underneath for the chair so your people aren't forced to sit with their legs glued together. Now let's talk about the condition of the desk. I would guess that 99.99 % of office workers would agree that the desk is very high on your *what's important to me* list. This has always been the case. The desk is a self-esteem issue as much as a necessity issue. So what is the condition of your employee's desk or workstation? Great? New? Decent? Terrible? Only you can answer that. If you are fortunate enough to have fairly new workstations or ones that are in beautiful condition, do whatever it takes to keep them that way. If they are *decent*, you might want to look at this improvement down the road. And if they truly fall into the *old and beaten-up* category, you need to look into an immediate change if at all possible. Many times I have witnessed companies who do not have the budget for state-of-the-art furniture but have invested in good used workstations that have changed the entire morale of the people in the center. Is it not like the automobile? Like me, how many of you have purchased a car that was not *brand new* but was new enough to you? Wasn't it wonderful to go from what you were driving to this newer car? A newer car made you feel special. The workstation is no different so don't underestimate how an investment in used or refurbished workstations can make a big difference to your workers. It's all relative. A step up is an improvement and therefore a morale booster, and therefore increases motivation.

Here's another consideration about the desk. Make sure that all the drawers work smoothly and properly. I don't know about you but I once had one of those desks where two of the drawers didn't close all the way and when I pushed either drawer in as far as it would go it was all cockeyed. And then it was hard to pull it back out because it no longer fit on the rollers properly. Probably some of you have been there too. Frustrating right? Aggravating? A pain in the A#@! If you can remember that, now remember the difference it made when you got a new desk that worked properly. Whether it was a replacement desk or new furniture at a new job or any change that was a step up, you felt like a kid with a new toy, right? Well your employees are no different. Times haven't changed the fact that little frustrations as

126

well as the big ones can be a major distraction to performance and productivity as well as an attitude destroyer.

Finally, make sure your employees have enough file space. While many operations use sophisticated automation that eliminates most of the paperwork, many do not. And even with automation there is the always some paperwork that needs to be filed properly, which means there's a need for file space. If the workstations do not have enough file space, make sure they have separate file cabinets. Otherwise you are just inviting the disorganization we spoke of earlier in this chapter that will ultimately result in less comfortable, less motivated and less successful people.

Adequate workspace, solid functional furniture that's in good condition and a comfortable chair are some of the tools that are not a luxury but a necessity for good results. Let's see if this memory helps to clarify the point. When you were growing up, did you have to do chores around the house like mowing the lawn, raking and bagging the leaves, doing the dishes, or sweeping the basement? If not, I wish I could have lived at your house. If so, can you remember the frustrations of a lawnmower that wouldn't start or maybe the blades weren't very sharp? Or the old rake that was missing a few teeth and kept leaving trails of leaves behind? Or the drain stopper that didn't fit exactly right so the sink or tub water would drain out? Or the broom with the terribly uneven bristles that made sweeping difficult, with an old dustpan that just didn't ever lay flat to the floor making it impossible to sweep everything up? Oh my gosh, I just thought of another one! The scissors-type hedge clippers that never got sharpened that made it so hard to clip the bushes. All of these examples hold two things in common. Number one, it made the job frustrating and harder than it had to be. And number two, the finished product showed disappointing results. I can still hear my father making the very same statement when he talked about the importance of supplying the resources necessary to do it. "Unless I give you the proper tools to do the job I'm asking you to do, I can't really expect your best effort or your very best results." How true, Dad. Give your people the tools they need to be motivated to make the best effort they can and more often than not you will get the results you wanted.

## PAINT, PICTURES and PLANTS

The combination of these three **P's** equals another **P**, **P**ositive attitudes. And positive attitudes result in two more **P's**, **P**erformance and **P**roductivity. It's amazing the way a cosmetically attractive office atmosphere can lift the overall morale and motivation in our industry. Well, maybe *amazing* is a strong word since we're talking again about self-esteem and having pride in where you work. *Dramatic* might be a better word. Maybe part of the issue is that unfortunately, the word *telemarketing* still carries a negative connotation. For many people, the words *telemarketing* or *telesales* paint a frightening image of some telemarketing *boiler room*, a smoke-filled office with people sitting elbow-to-elbow at long folding tables, tearing pages out of telephone books for leads as they make cold calls and try to shove something down people throats.

Aside from this lingering industry reputation, the fact remains that when your environment is freshly painted, has clean carpet or flooring, and the department is nicely decorated with pictures and plants, employees feel more positive about their work environment and are far more motivated to do a good job. While I believe this is true for any work environment I know it's true in our industry. And don't give me the old excuse here that your workplace "can't look good because it's an older environment." Old doesn't mean bad. Furthermore, old doesn't have to mean bad. It just takes a little creativity on your part and a little company cash to make a huge difference.

I think I mentioned that I once managed a telesales environment that was, how-you-say, less than conducive to maximum performance due to being cosmetically rough. I knew the environment was negatively affecting me as well as my staff. I got the company to commit to a few unbudgeted dollars, organized what I called a weekend workday and then went to my staff for help. It was a simple presentation; whatever time they could offer on the specified Saturday, they would help transform our demoralizing environment into a newer looking, freshly painted atmosphere. While not everyone volunteered, we had a great turnout. Everyone worked hard all day painting, hanging pictures and posters, neatly arranging documentation in every workstation and strategically placing plants and other knick-knacks to top it off. I supplied hamburgers and fries for lunch, pizzas for a late afternoon snack, and beverages throughout the day. As it turned out, some of the employees brought baked goods and snacks, as well as some of their own tools and painting supplies and it was a huge success. And the impact that it had on our entire office was even bigger. When everyone arrived for work on Monday, the ones that didn't help were amazed and the ones that had done it all appreciated it more! People started feeling much better about being there. I noticed more people having their families meet them there since they were no longer embarrassed about how it looked. And the company saw an increase in performance. Just a coincidence? Not a chance.

The beauty of what we did was that it didn't involve a big expense because we did most of the work ourselves. Maybe some of you have done something similar. Maybe this will inspire you to discover the difference a simple coat of paint can make. If you've ever repainted an older car, your old outdoor furniture, a bicycle, or an old fence, you've seen the difference. There's a wonderful feeling of gratification when you see the new, freshly painted look. You just feel better driving it, sitting in it, riding it, or just looking at it.

Pictures and posters also uplift an environment. I'm not saying you have to order large expensive framed motivational posters from supply houses or go to expensive framing stores. I've been in positions where the budget won't cover it. What you can do is go to a discount department store like K-Mart and buy motivational posters for under $5 and frames for $20 and you're set to go. Another great source for posters and banners is teacher supply stores. My wife has to restrain me when I visit these stores. They're a gold mine for colorful positive banners that highlight success, attitude and teamwork, all sold at inexpensive prices. Pick up a roll of double-sided tape and once again you've installed some instant improvement. Believe me, as the pictures and posters go up, so will employee morale.

Decorating with plants can be the icing on the cake. While renting plants from a nursery can be costly and impractical, purchasing plants and getting professional help to care for them is not. *Professional help* means one or two of your employees *who know how to care for plants*. And as you will read in an upcoming chapter, here is a perfect opportunity for additional responsibility and leadership roles. Always select a team of several people to cover for absence or vacation, and give them the responsibility of taking care of the plants. While you supply all the necessary materials (soil, ingredients, etc.) they supply the most important factor, the proper *attention*. What a great story line here. Your environment will look better with plants that are nurtured by your own employees who are further motivated by the additional responsibility you've given them to take care of plants for your department. Pretty good scenario, I'd say.

## TEMPERATURE

Temperature? Right about now you're probably thinking, "We need to take Dave Worman's *temperature*, he's got to be sick!" What does temperature have to do with motivation? While I admit this is probably not the strongest motivating factor that comes to mind, it does carry some weight and is certainly worthy of discussion when we are looking at work environment as the overall non-monetary motivator that it is.

What is the current temperature in your work environment? Is it 65 degrees . . . 70 degrees . . . 80? Do you even know? While you may not know, your people do. And it's a lot more important to them than you may think. Once again, we're discussing the importance of the comfort zone and how it affects concentration levels. Concentration levels certainly have a bearing on the success of your people, right? Well, the room temperature is an important element in their comfort zone and therefore affects their ability to concentrate.

Remember in school when it was too hot in class how hard it was not to stay alert while the teacher was talking? How about in church while the pastor is preaching the sermon but it's so hot that everyone is fanning themselves? Hard to pay attention, right? Ever been to a sporting event when it's so cold that you can hardly watch what's happening on the field? I think this is a common experience, uncomfortable temperatures are barriers to concentration.

Likewise, the temperature comfort zone applies directly to your telemarketing/telesales environment. What is the temperature in your work area? Is it too hot? Too cold? And what defines too hot or too cold? During consulting assignments I have visited companies where the work climate was like the Amazon Jungle or the North Pole. Don't fall for the theories that "warm is more comfortable" or "chill 'em and they'll stay awake." An extreme on either end is just that, *extreme.* You don't need people sweating profusely and you definitely don't need icicles hanging from the ceiling or people wearing their coats and gloves. While I don't care for the word impossible, it is *almost* impossible to concentrate in extreme room temperatures on either end of the thermometer. And the other obvious wrinkle to the question is "How do I make everyone happy I've got an easy answer for you. You can't and you won't. Management 101 tells us that one of the worst mistakes we can make as leaders is to attempt to please everyone because you can never do it. But let's think sensibly here and evaluate what represents the most balanced temperature. I have always found that 70 to 73 degrees will capture the best comfort zone for the majority of people. You'll always have a few people who think it's too cold or too hot. But when you move outside of this range, the number of unhappy people rises.

Also you need to be careful that employees do not have access to the thermostats or major problems are in your immediate future. When employees can adjust the temperature, cut off air conditioning, turn up the heat or change any variation of temperature control, the game of *musical temperatures* begins. And this is one of those games that is not fun. Do your employees play this game in your work area? One employee comes in feeling cold so he turns off the air conditioning and in some cases, turns the heat on. And soon another employee is perspiring from the heat and he goes back and switches the air to colder. And the game continues, from the equator to the Arctic Circle. Back and forth. I've seen it range from under 60 to over 85 degrees. Sound familiar? Not only does the room temperature swing back and forth but so does the dialogue between the employees who are doing the changing. And if you haven't heard these conversations, I promise you the dialogue doesn't include "Thank you for changing that." Obviously, this causes great problems. Employees who are cold and want to be warm get upset with the employees who turn off the heat and turn on the air and vice-versa. You can avoid this unhealthy situation by putting clear lock boxes over all your thermostats if necessary and distributing communication that forbids staff employees from tampering with thermostats in any way, shape or form. Very simply, the game of *musical temperatures* is over. Limit the number of keys to these boxes to a select few and your problem is solved.

I hope that the last few pages have done at least one of the following two things. First, I hope it reminded or showed you the importance of the *work environment* to the motivation of your telephone professionals. Remember that our job as leaders is not actually to motivate our employees. As we discussed early in the book, motivation according to Webster is *something from within that prompts or incites an action*. Remember too, that *old* doesn't mean *bad*. If you, like many, are not enjoying the luxury of a brand new environment, then accept that it's not new and that it's okay. Just stir the old creative juices and get them flowing. A work environment that has undergone a facelift will often uplift the employees more than the spoils of a new environment. Why? It can actually mean more to people who take the *guts* of something old and solid and help transform it into looking new. If I had the choice of a brand new Corvette or the 1963 split-window Classic that had been completely refurbished, it would be an easy choice to take the '63. How about you? Many times the restored and refurbished feels more valuable than the brand new. So look back at the Paint, Pictures, and Plants section of this chapter, add a little imagination and just a few dollars and get ready for some major results. Motivation comes from within. Our job as leaders is not to motivate people but to create an environment where self-motivation can be nurtured. Providing an environment that looks good, has comfortable workspace and furniture and a well-balanced temperature will create an atmosphere more conducive to positivity, motivation and subsequently, more success. Their job is hard enough; the least we can do is give them a decent environment that doesn't present extra obstacles.

Let me close with one final thought. You are leaders in an industry where burnout is high and turnover is often. You know this to be true because before becoming leaders you too experienced the redundant work of being on the phone. Remember to give due attention to the quality of your environment. If you underestimate this, you'll also be underestimating the negative consequences of your oversight.

# 10

# Job Titles

L et's begin with the questions I can already hear you thinking. What's in a title, you ask? And how much importance does it really hold? The answer to both questions is plenty! And while this chapter may not include plenty of words, it most definitely holds plenty of importance. There is plenty in a title, and it means plenty to people. When we talk about job titles, we're talking about self-esteem. The dictionary defines self-esteem as Belief in oneself, self-respect; pride. The way someone thinks he is perceived in the workplace is a critical component to overall attitude and morale. Now we've done it, right? We brought up attitude and morale. These might be the two biggest factors affecting the ability to perform. And both can be positively or negatively affected by something as seemingly trivial as a job title.

In our industry, the word telemarketing used to almost be a cuss word. Yes, let's be honest. In some arenas it probably still is. The history of our profession included the practice of interrupting people during supper. It depended on poor demographics to identify real prospects. It involved credit card fraud. And it used rude, unethical sales tactics or "teleconning" as we called it, as well as a host of other negative associations, some valid and some invalid. As a result, many people turn sour when they hear the word. This is a shame because telemarketing is the perfect word for our industry, marketing by the telephone. Back in the real world, if your employees are embarrassed by the reputation of their livelihood, this will negatively affect their self-esteem and in general, the way they feel about themselves, their position and how they perform their job. These feelings usually lead to a decrease in morale and consequently, productivity. And the only thing that will increase in this situation is employee turnover.

Picture this common situation. Your employees are engaged in conversation with friends at church, the grocery store, at a party, a sporting event or the mall, and guess what subject always comes up? Work. No matter how the conversation starts or how many people are involved or the place or the time of day, the subject of employment always comes up. You know the questions. "Where you working now?" "Are you still with (company name)? And then come the questions that hit home. "What do you actually do?" and/or "What's your title?" People usually respond with their job title or something similar unless they want to avoid the subject. And the only reason anyone would try to avoid the subject is out of embarrassment or shame. Do you want your people feeling embarrassed or ashamed of where they work or what they do? Obviously not, and it doesn't have to be that way. You can help make them feel good about who they are and what they do with a job title that makes them proud.

Remember our discussion in the last chapter about the importance of pride in the success of our people? Well, here is an easy way for you to create and maintain some positive motivation within your people. The following four titles are often used in our industry that have replaced the typical and unsatisfactory Telemarketing Rep:

1. SALES ASSOCIATE
2. SALES CONSULTANT
3. ACCOUNT SPECIALIST
4. ACCOUNT EXECUTIVE

When you read these four examples, I'm sure you're wondering if anyone really uses these titles or if they're really that different than Telemarketing Rep, or whether any of these really fit your people, or even what they mean. We'll address each of these questions.

What do they mean? They're really not supposed to mean anything different than the title you're currently using. It's just a different way of saying it. For instance, if your employees are selling over the phone but do not have their own account base, Sales Associate or Sales Consultant would be a perfect description. Would that not make them feel a little worthier than Telemarketing Rep or Telemarketer? I'm pretty sure it would. While these two titles can also be used with inside sales positions where employees do have their own customer base, Account Specialist or Account Executive are appropriate in these situations as well. Telemarketing Rep or Telemarketer describes an employee who has no responsibilities other than staying on the phone, making 400 calls per day in a redundant, repetitive atmosphere. In most telemarketing environments whether independent or corporate, this job includes other activities such as administrative duties, filing, mailing out information, filling out order forms, surveys, questionnaires, appointment forms, interoffice phone calls, and interfacing with other departments. Any combination of these tasks and responsibilities makes your employees more than just a telemarketer.

For years now I have used the title Account Executive for my telephone professionals and it seems to be popular and well appreciated. These positions included customer or account bases and the employees have to research records, past sales and other information. I guess I could have simply left it at Telemarketing Rep. But you should have seen how excited they were to get their new business cards that said Account Executive. The other work they do definitely qualifies them to be called Account Executive and the title makes them feel better about themselves.

If your environment is related to telemarketing functions other than sales such as customer service, collections, surveys or others, you can be equally creative with your titles as you are with sales. Customer Service Associate or Collections Specialist are just a couple of examples of how to improve the motivational mileage you can get out of titles other then rep. Not everyone needs to be a rep; in fact at this point rep might as well stand for REPetitious because too many people use it way too often.

Along with Account Executive, I have also used the other three titles and can personally vouch for all four regarding the way they make employees feel about who they are at work. Now let's return to the same scenario about the conversation that turns to the subject of work. But this time, your people are proud of their titles and whom they work for. Instead of answering "What do you do at work?" with sidetracking questions like "Hey, how 'bout those Red Sox?" they'll speak openly and proudly about their jobs and in many cases hand out their business cards. Which way do you want your employees to respond to this question? While the answer is obvious, have you taken any steps to insure that your employees will be able to respond positively? Maybe your people are already able to answer those questions with their heads held high. If that's the case, I commend you. And if not yet, that's okay. A better question would be, will you take any necessary steps to insure their positive reaction? Remember that knowledge doesn't help you if you don't use it. The application of knowledge is what makes it powerful.

In some larger companies or corporations, employee job descriptions are put under a job classification system that determines wages and in some cases, titles. Two of my corporate positions use this system and this makes it a little tricky to change titles. But it can still be done. I met with Human Resources in both companies with the job descriptions of the current Telemarketing Representative and we discussed two

137

issues. First I explained why the job descriptions (which included activities other than phone time) deserved a different title. And second, I explained how giving them new, more meaningful titles would make a motivational difference. I was able to make a case for both points. I believe that my request was granted because the material was in place and especially because of the presentation. Put your sales caps on, leaders, and sell Human Resources on the advantage of this change.

**Note:** In these job classification systems, title changes can often mean a new classification and therefore more money. Be sure you preface your conversation or presentation with the fact that you are merely requesting title changes not merit increases. This will definitely get you off to a more convincing start. However if you are involved with a process that includes pay increases for everyone in your department, this makes an ideal time to also make a title change if possible.

The bottom line is that when you are dealing with job titles you are dealing with pride. And pride promotes a positive attitude, and a positive attitude is the foundation for continued success. Be different and creative with your job titles whenever possible and you'll end up being the leader of a much happier and more positive, productive, profitable and motivated environment.

# 11

# Theme Contests

My belief in the power of telemarketing contests is no secret. And obviously I am not alone. While I was confident about getting a good response to my first book, *Motivating with Sales Contests*, I was unprepared for what actually happened. It was surprising to get so many calls from readers who just wanted to say hello and talk about their success after implementing ideas from the book. But I was quite surprised when the calls started coming from countries all over the world. The requests ranged from additional book orders to people just wanting further advice on a particular section of the book. And collectively, the calls had one common denominator. From Germany, Japan, Great Britain, Australia, Canada, Brazil, Mexico, and Sweden, from everywhere came one universal confirmation. "Thank you Dave, we needed this book in our industry! Contests work!" But that's no news flash to me, I know contests work, but it was inspiring and exciting to hear the same enthusiasm from all corners of the world. This was also apparent whenever I presented seminars at national conferences. Often there were groups from other nations who listened through their interpreters, and it always tickled me when I would hear expressions of laughter or excitement long after I covered a point because it took the interpreter a few minutes to translate.

Before we continue, let's talk about what I mean when I say contests work? In this case, we can define working as producing elevated levels of motivation, higher levels of all forms of productivity and therefore producing higher profitability. Ultimately, working means producing higher levels of overall success. Beyond the statistics, contests generate enthusiasm, excitement and a healthy sense of competition. And most of all, contests are just flat-out fun!

Contests have always worked, they are currently working and they will forever work. The call function is irrelevant. Business to business, business to consumer, outbound or inbound, it doesn't matter. If your environment conducts any type of business by phone, contests work. And I've certainly learned from the response to my first book that contests work no matter what language you speak. And while many successful contests include cash prizes, you can also create contests that raise enthusiasm, motivation, productivity and profitability without offering a cash prize. Yes, that's right. I did say no cash and that the contests would work. Here's how. You can create theme contests. These contests highlight certain events, holidays or activities. They allow employees to dress a little different than the norm and create a chance to decorate the office with some relevant props and decorations. That's exactly why these contests are so much fun and so successful. Let's consider four ideas for theme contests that I have used over the years and examples that you can use right away.

## 1. HOLIDAYS

Holidays are a natural theme for contests since one of the most important elements for a successful theme contest is already in place—the atmosphere. Because people are already aware of the significance of each holiday, you can ease them into contest mode using the holiday as the contest theme. Here are a couple of holiday contest examples that I have used with great success almost every year.

## Pot of gold

*St. Patrick's Day*

- **Contest Description:** Individual employees are awarded with shamrocks for reaching performance goals and they try to win the *pot of gold*.

- **Contest Guidelines:** TSRs (Telephone Sales Reps) collect green shamrocks (purchase these or cut them out of construction paper) for reaching predetermined calling goals. At day's end all shamrocks are signed by the employees and go into a pot for a drawing. Three lucky shamrocks are drawn to determine the winners.

- **Prize(s):** The *Pot of Gold* is a plastic pot filled with gold-covered chocolate coins and time-off coupons.

- **Special Tips:** Announce a casual dress day encouraging the color green. Bonus shamrocks can also be earned if any employee paperwork includes any affiliated names or numbers (Green, 17, 317, Pat, Patrick, gold, etc.).

## Trick or treat

*Halloween*

- **Contest Description:** For reaching predetermined calling goals, a TSR tries to identify the mystery person on the posters that are covered with adhesive notes.

- **Contest Guidelines:** Purchase two celebrity posters and cover them with straight lines of small 1.5" x 2" self-sticking notes. Label one of them the *black* poster and the other one the *orange* poster. Put the covered posters up in the most visible areas of your department. For reaching predetermined calling goals, the employees pick from a large plastic pumpkin filled with candy wrapped in *orange* or *black* paper. The color of the wrapper determines from which poster board the person may now pull off a self-sticking note. The self-sticking notes act as a mask covering the identity of a famous person.

141

The employee now gets to guess the person *behind the mask*. This continues throughout the shift or day until someone wins.

- **Prize(s):** Bags of candy favorites (Milky Ways, Snickers, etc.) along with coupons for time off.
- **Special Tips:** Encourage your employees to wear Halloween costumes (that don't interfere with their jobs) and have a costume-judging competition at break time. Winner gets to pull additional notes from the posters. Also be sure to turn the posters upside down or sideways before covering them with notes. This will add some much-needed confusion as they try to identify the posters.

These are only two examples of holiday theme contests. Think of all the creative ways you could develop contests around other holidays. The possibilities are endless. I always run a week- long contest prior to Christmas where employees put ornaments on our department Christmas tree for reaching productivity levels, attempting to win a special present. It's great fun. Our Christmas tree gets decorated throughout the week by all of the employees. On Thanksgiving, my contest rewards a few winners with a turkey for their Thanksgiving Day meal. And I promise you, productivity *explodes* in my July 4th contest called *Fireworks* where everyone wears red, white and blue. I also have an Easter egg hunt each year by putting different colored jelly beans in plastic Easter eggs. And I watch everyone's performance rise as they try to find the special colors of jellybeans that mean special prizes. Do you see what I mean? The possibilities are endless. To make these holiday contests as effective as possible, note the following suggestions:

- Add props and decorations to reinforce the theme atmo phere

142

- Get everyone in the holiday spirit by dressing accordingly
- Always run the contest prior to the holiday and as close to the holiday as possible. Once a holiday has passed, so has your opportunity for gathering enthusiasm.

You have many opportunities each year to celebrate holidays with special theme contests for boosting motivation. Get your calendar out, pre-plan as many contests as you can and most of all have fun.

## 2. ANNIVERSARIES

While there are fewer anniversaries than holidays, famous anniversary dates present some good opportunities for theme contests. You'll need the same elements here as for the holiday contest, like decorations and props and giving advance notice so people can anticipate and plan on dressing accordingly. Timing is also important but unlike some holidays you will probably be able to hold your contest on the exact anniversary date. If this isn't possible remember to hold it before the day as close to the actual date as possible. Following is one example of an anniversary date contest that I have run on numerous occasions with great success.

### Journey to the moon

*NASA space program's first walk on the moon, July 1969*

■ **Contest Description:** Hitting performance goals creates *fuel* for each team space shuttle in quest of a safe landing on the moon.

■ **Contest Guidelines:** Break your employees into teams of astronauts. Use a   poster board or dry erase board to draw up the course the space shuttles must earn   to get to the moon. Successfully reaching predetermined performance goals  moves the team space shuttle in position to land on the moon. The first team shuttle to make

143

a safe landing on the moon wins.
- **Prize(s):** Winning team of the astronauts gets a pizza and time-off coupons (to rest). And the astronaut who provides the *most fuel* wins a special prize.
- **Special Tips:** Make sure your managers and supervisors are positioned properly as *Houston / NASA* to help guide the team space shuttles through the contest. Additional *fuel* id earned if any employee paperwork includes any anniversary affiliated names or numbers (1969, 720, moon, Neil or Armstrong).

Put on your thinking caps and come up with some other creative ideas. It's just one more opportunity to create some motivation around a special date. And by the way, you'll also create some extra productivity. Would you care for some?

### 3. SPORTS

If it's nighttime and your eyes are drooping or you're due in a meeting in a few minutes, stop reading. Put the book down and come back to it later when you are fresh and unhurried. This section is far too important to read with half-opened eyes or rush through in a hurry. As far as theme contests go, sports offers the widest range of possibilities and in my experience generates the most successful contests. Why sports? I can sum it up in one word, *competition*. And I've always loved hearing people analyze other people with comments like "she's very competitive," or "he's too competitive," or other critical statements. Whenever I hear this I always want to ask, "And what about you?" The truth is that we're all competitive by nature. And while the tendency to compete comes in different sizes, we're all born with it. I'm not making a judgment. I realize that some people like to win more than others do. I'm simply stating the fact that no one enters a competition thinking, "It'll be fun if I lose."
The competitive spirit is in all of us. And that's what makes

144

sports such a natural feeding ground for theme contests. The competitive spirit will surface during any contest. But somehow when you have teams and base the contest on some sports event, there's extra adrenaline. Even with people who are not sports fans, this phenomenon just happens.

There are so many options here. Football, baseball, basketball, golf, car racing—I've used them all. And while a sports theme can always be successful, a major sporting event will jump it to a higher level. Some of my most successful contests ever were structured around the Super Bowl, the NBA Finals, the NCAA Final Four, the World Series, the Masters or U.S. Open, the Indianapolis 500 and the all-star games. These carry an extra punch because the buzz about the big event is already in the air. It's not much of a stretch to harness the enthusiasm and cash in. Here are a few examples of sports contests that have always been successful:

### TSR football

- **Contest Description:** Two teams square off against each other and gain offensive yardage toward touchdowns by reaching calling goals.

- **Contest Guidelines:** Divide the work shift/day into two halves with a break or lunchtime representing *half time*. As employees reach the goals [that you've determined] they produce offensive yardage toward touchdowns worth seven points each. Keep score on a big white dry erase board for everyone to see. The highest scoring team at day's end is the winner.

- **Prize(s):** Pizza and time-off coupons for all members of the winning team. The MVP (Most Valuable Player) goes to the most offensive yardage on either team. Award is a small trophy and if possible, tickets to a local football game.

- **Special Tips:** Use a cap gun to end the first half and the game. Encourage employees to dress in team colors, post

145

a scoreboard and use any appropriate props and decorations. Managers and supervisors can wear referee shirts and use whistles appropriately.

Another version of TSR (Telephone Sales Rep) Football is to cover a five- or six-foot folding table with a strip of green indoor/outdoor carpeting. This is an inexpensive, one-time purchase you can use over and over again. Using masking tape, measure and tape off yard lines and mark them 10, 20, 30, etc., with a black magic marker. Then go to your local sports card or sporting goods store and get bumper stickers for two teams. Peel them and stick them in each end zone. With very little time and money invested, you've got a beautiful and realistic football field. Using a small toy football (start it on a 50-yard line), move it the proper yardage whenever someone earns it. Let the team move the ball the appropriate yardage based on your guidelines. The ball will go back and forth, up and down the field until someone scores. Put the ball back on the 50-yard line and go again. They love to go up to the field in front of everyone else and move the ball forward. It's a blast!

TSR Football works best around the Super Bowl or any big local pro or college football rivalry. While the Super Bowl is always a winner, some of my football contests based on rivalries drive more interest, more intensity, more fun, and yes, more productivity. It probably carries more punch when it's closer to home. My Cincinnati Bengals vs. Cleveland Browns or Ohio State vs. Michigan or Alabama vs. Auburn contests have almost always been more successful than my contest based on the Super Bowl. Of course, if your home team is in the Super Bowl, you've got it made.

### TSR basketball

■ **Contest Description:** A team-oriented contest where employees from both teams   earn the right to shoot at a real toy basketball hoop from one, two or three-point range.

- **Contest Guidelines:** Divide your people into two teams. Assign a coach for each team to act as cheerleaders. Reaching individual productivity or performance goals earns attempts at one, two or three-point baskets. Break time or lunch hour is halftime. The highest scoring team at shift or day's end is the winner.
- **Prize(s):** Pizza meal and time-off coupons for winning team. MVP (most points) is awarded a small trophy and if possible, tickets to a local basketball game.
- **Special Tips:** Have managers and supervisors where referee shirts and equip them with whistles. Use any form of toy basketball hoop (Little Tykes works best). Also, add any possible appropriate props and decorations to help make the atmosphere more authentic.

Whenever running this contest or any variation, I set up my Little Tykes basketball hoop and have great success around the NBA all-star game, the NBA Finals, the NCAA Final Four or, like football, any big local rivalries. All the same elements are in place, it's just basketball, not football. Be sure to always set up a one-point line because some people are embarrassed to try a two- or three-point shot but will gladly try from a shorter distance.

## TGA golf
*(Telemarketing Golf Association)*

- **Contest Description:** Hitting predetermined performance and productivity goals allows employees to putt in front of everyone and compete for the tournament trophy.
- **Contest Guidelines:** For reaching goals, employees get to walk up the fairway to attempt a putt on the green (use a 15-foot strip of green indoor/outdoor carpet and a put-

147

ting return device for the hole. Each employee chooses the length of the putt he or she would like to attempt:

15 feet = EAGLE (-2)
12 feet = BIRDIE (-1)
8 feet = PAR (EVEN)
**Note:** If *any putt is missed*, it counts as a *bogie* (+1)
The employee with the lowest score at shift/day's end wins the tournament and the trophy.

■ **Prize(s):** Winner receives small golf trophy and time-off coupons. Greens fees to local golf course or gift certificate from a golf equipment store also works well.

■ **Special Tips:** Authorize a casual dress day with golf attire recommended. Add any possible props and decorations for the authentic atmosphere and any administrative assistant or secretary who is going to help facilitate this contest should dress as a caddy.

This format resembles a regular PGA event. I have also had great success using teams of two, three or four players. They aim for a combined low score and you can post their scores as a twosome, threesome or foursome. This generates mutual encouragement and team spirit. The advantage about TGA golf is that while not everyone can shoot baskets, most people have been putt-putt golfing at least once in their lives so they know how to do it. I have found that the most successful time to run this contest is during the Masters, the U.S. Open or, if you are local, to another PGA event. I have run this during the World Series of Golf that is played at the Firestone Country Club in Akron, Ohio because it was local to us. As in basketball, make sure to put one line for putts fairly close so those who are shy can have a chance.

These are just a few examples of sports theme contests. You can run a baseball contest around the all-star game, the playoffs or the World Series for runs instead of points. Put up a few team pennants and caps, get your umpire's mask and have fun. I have often run a contest on the Friday prior to the Indianapolis 500 using a folding table laid out as the course. I draw it on poster boards with measurement distances and tape those to the table. I use matchbox cars and break the division into *crews* and have a great time finding out who will get the *checkered flag*. Have a special guest announce, "Ladies and gentlemen . . . start your engines!" And you're off! In smaller departments I have sometimes have them compete as individuals instead of teams.

The Olympics is another great theme for short-term or longterm contests. Just use your imagination. I always tape record the Olympic song off the television and then play it every morning before starting the day. Also be sure to get some gold, silver and bronze medals (fake, of course) and play or have someone sing our national anthem during the award ceremonies.

There are so many things you can do using a variety of sports themes throughout the year. Be sure to focus on props and costumes that beef up the authenticity of the environment. And most of all join in personally any way you can.

## 4. MISCELLANEOUS

Finally, use miscellaneous ideas for theme contests. Once or twice a year I use *50s/60s Day* (and it's often requested more). This time frame is one of the most nostalgic and popular in our history, especially since the *baby boomers* dominated the population. Memorabilia includes music from American pop to the British invasion and muscle cars. Major influences from the entertainment world, the rise and fall and loss of prominent political figures, the emergence of the space program, and memorable moments in sports make these decades a favorite even among people who weren't born then. Following is one version of this contest:

## 50s/60s day

- ■ **Contest Description:** A 1950s/1960s era contest where employees earn points by reaching predetermined goals throughout the day and answering trivia questions related to the time period. Bonus points for best dressed.
- ■ **Contest Guidelines:** Employees earn 50 points for reaching predetermined productivity goals. With each 50 points comes a trivia question from the 50s/60s (correct answer doubles your points). Spontaneous trivia questions will be asked throughout the day for bonus points. At break time or lunch hour those wearing period dress will be judged for bonus points. First place = 110 points (50 + 60); second place = 60 points; third place = 50 points. At the end of the day, the employees with the top three point totals win. Encourage employees to dress accordingly.
- ■ **Prize(s):** Winners receive tapes or CDs and time-off coupons. Award the overall winner with a gift certificate to a theme-related restaurant like Hard Rock Café or Johnny Rocketts.
- ■ **Special Tips:** Put together a fun promotional flyer prior to the contest and hand it out early to get everyone in the mood. If possible, play music throughout the day from the 1950s and 1960s. Put up props and decorations related to this era (you can pick up some good ones inexpensively at any party supply store).

I have also run several variations of this theme, including me as the disc jockey spinning my stacks of wax throughout the day. Playing music from Chuck Berry, Buddy Holly, Sam Cooke, Elvis, The Beatles, The Supremes, The Rolling Stones, The Byrds, Jefferson Airplane, and Cream, we rock 'n' roll all day. Encourage your people to get out the old peg-leg jeans, poodle skirts, shades and penny loafers, and the bell-bottoms, tie-dyed tee shirts, sandals and peace necklaces. And I always create a fun information flyer to give everyone prior to the contest to get them in the right mood.

You can also have a Western Day where everyone dresses in jeans, cowboy hats, boots and chaps. Set up your productivity standards to equal horses' broken, steers branded or notches in the gun belt and have a great day. When you use your imagination, you'll come up with many themes I haven't even mentioned. Theme contests are favorites because they include dressing up and because they're reserved for special occasions. Following are summary tips for running the best theme contests. I may have touched on most of these earlier but they're worth repeating.

- Whenever possible, encourage people to dress accordingly. This could mean holiday colors (orange and black for Halloween) or team colors for sports events, the 50s/60s look or Western wear. The more participation, the more fun. And the more fun, the more successful.

- If you can get them, take the time to hang up theme props and decorations. This adds to the atmosphere of the contest. And remember this involves creativity more than expenses. I'm still using some of the same 50s/60s decorations I bought in 1987 when I first ran this contest! And back then they cost less than $10. I use the same football field for college and pro games, changing the end zone bumper stickers to designate the teams. And I use the same team pennants and caps every time. Am I getting through to you here? If you have to invest in anything, it is normally a one-time purchase. And in the long run it's not a cost, it's an investment. Believe me, you'll cover your cost. Some of the decorations are easy to make. Just give a little thought to creating an authentic atmosphere for any given contest and I'm sure you'll see what I mean.

151

- Give away prizes related to the contest theme whenever possible. Remember that we're not talking about handing out cash. I've given away tickets to sporting events for TSR Football/Basketball/Baseball, dinner for two at the Hard Rock Cafe or tapes and CDs on 50s/60s Day, certificates to Lone Star Steakhouse on Western day, and bags of candy on Halloween. Whenever you do this, you strengthen the theme of the contest, which again adds to the spirit and fun.
- Always remind your staff that contests, especially theme-based contests (because they usually include decorations, props, special dress, etc.) can be fun but also need to be productive. Tell them that if the contests rank high in fun and low in productivity, you can't run it again because it doesn't represent a benefit to the company. Because the employees enjoy these contests so much, they will generally work harder and show more productivity than normal so they can continue having them. This puts the responsibility on them, and they'll always come through.

Theme contests will create an epidemic of enthusiasm in your telemarketing environment. And in case you haven't figured it out yet, that means an epidemic of motivation, which will result in an epidemic of success.

---

**NOTE:** If you would like to order a copy of my first book *Motivating with Sales Contests: The Complete Guide to Motivating Your Telephone Professionals with Contests that Produce Record Breaking Results,* call 800-326-7721, or 402-895-9399, or visit www.businessbyphone.com.

# 12

# Additional Responsibility

There are probably employees in your organization that are capable of handling extra responsibility and would welcome something more. I know you're probably cringing as you think of some of your people. I'm certainly not talking about everyone but too many telemarketing managers, trainers and supervisors don't realize two important facts. First, there are people who are ready for additional responsibility and second, you should be giving them the chance, which will boost their motivation. This may not sound logical to you. Since when do people become motivated by extra work? Well, first of all I didn't say extra responsibility meant extra work. In many cases the additional responsibility replaces time portions of regular duties. And secondly, if it does involve extra work, most people don't mind if it is added responsibility and not just more work. These two are totally different. Extra work on its own is not much of an incentive to anyone. Additional responsibility that brings extra work of a more accountable nature is acceptable. This means a chance to have something other employees don't have, to be special, to be somehow more important, to be noticed. When you look at it from that perspective, now you realize why this is not only be acceptable but can be desirable.

As leaders, our job is twofold. We must first identify these people and then we should match their strengths with the appropriate responsibilities. Let's consider each of these tasks. First, how do we identify these responsibility seekers? Asking good questions during individual meetings and review sessions will help you pick them out. And naturally, you should observe your employees for qualifying characteristics such as dependability, maturity and solid work ethics. Consider whether they ask good questions and whether they offer to help out beyond their own duties. And obviously, you should look at the quality of their performance records. First, if their performance or productivity falls short, there is no reason to consider them taking on more. Second, if any type of training is going to be a part of the additional responsibility, why would you want them training other people when their own performance doesn't set a good example? And why would other employees want to be trained by someone whose own performance is weak? In addition, you should ask yourself whether this person could really handle the added responsibility you have in mind? Is it a good fit for them and for me? You might also want to meet with any level of subordinate managers or supervisors (if you have any) and discuss the responsibility at hand, who might be a good fit and why, who deserves it and why and any other relevant factors.

Furthermore, whenever you are considering expanding someone's responsibility, make sure he (she) is worthy. Make sure he deserves it. Make sure he can handle it. In other words, don't do what I have done a few too many times, giving an undeserving employee extra responsibility because I thought it was the remedy he needed to step up and do better. Have you made this mistake too? You see someone struggling and by playing psychologist, you conclude that giving him more responsibility will make him a better, more productive employee? Well, if you have you probably ended up kicking yourself in the pants just as I did for this managerial blunder. Maybe you learned after doing it once. I didn't! No sir, old Dave made the same mistake many times (*many* meaning I'm too embarrassed to tell you the number!).

If you promote an undeserving employee you are doing an injustice to yourself, the employee and your work environment. You won't get what you needed and the undeserving employee will fall further behind in his regular tasks. And furthermore, the more deserving employees will be disappointed and even angered by your selection. Face it, you can't win so don't do it. Take the time to analyze every piece of the puzzle before choosing the right person. And here's a final tip for the identification process: listen and watch. Listen to your people and watch them. Many times they will give you clues that they are interested in more responsibility but we, as leaders are not hearing them. If you, yourself can't take on this role and have a subordinate team of leaders who are closer to the day-to-day activities, make sure they are listening and watching. If you don't, you're missing some easy opportunities for non-monetary motivation.

Now let's take a look at some ideas for the responsibility itself. Following are some ideas I have implemented in my work environments that have always been effective. You'll probably find that some of these are practical in your environment while others are not. These may also ignite some ideas of your own that are well suited to your own department or company. Let's begin.

## TRAINING

Believing in the theory (no, the fact) that training never ends, training provides the best opportunity for added responsibility that also ends up motivating your chosen employees. Please don't get caught up in the old ego trap here that says only managers can provide training. Some of the best training I've ever done has included the help of my employees. Consider any form of spot training on skills-based issues like closing the sale, answering objections and general telephone techniques. Then, as we discussed a few minutes ago, analyze who would

155

be a good fit for this leadership role. This should not be tough to figure out. You or your managers must know which employees are strong in different areas. After you've chosen someone, work out ways he can assist you in the training. And always share the importance of the training and the positive things that are going to happen because of his assistance. This isn't rocket science here. Oh, and by the way, get ready for the motivational juices to stir as soon as you ask him to take this on. His mind will go wild. "Who me? Help train others? Be off the phone for awhile? Me, helping you lead a special lunchtime training session? This is awesome, everyone's going to be so envious." These thoughts continue until Barney Fife from the old *Andy Griffith Show* jumps into his body and takes over. "Yeah, well, now that I think about it, I probably am right for the job, I guess they finally saw my real potential." And he continues to entertain other *Fife* feelings of extreme self-confidence. All of these feelings come from pure and simple pride. People are proud to have the opportunity and that's what makes it so motivational. The level of involvement is up to you. I have used a wide range of responsibility, from having someone up there beside me to giving an employee's perspective on an area of training that I am conducting, all the way through the employee leading the entire training session without me. Again, you've got to determine the employee's capabilities. And I can give you a few specific examples of how deserving employees have helped me with training.

I have often held a training session on closing skills during initial training of new employees. This normally includes overheads, handouts and a generic look at how to close sales. And when I discuss how to apply those skills to our products and services, I have a special employee join me to look more deeply at the specifics of closing of our customers. The new employees have received general training and reminders on closing skills from me and are now going to get the benefit of a real pro when it comes to applying the skills to our products and services. And who else could do it better? Is there anyone better qualified than one of your best salespeople who excels at closing sales? I don't think so. And by the way, this approach is perceived as a benefit to your new employees. I can't begin to tell you how many of my employees have thanked me and told me how much they appreciate a current veteran of the trenches sitting with them before they get started. I realize that you've probably been on the phone in the past. So was I, so what? The point is that your chosen employee is still on the phone now and is one of your most successful people. Again, who could be better at relating to the new people and telling them exactly how to do it?

**CAUTION:** Here's a reminder. Now you can understand why the employee selection process is so important. Can you imagine your future problems if you choose someone to do this training that is successful but is doing it the wrong way? This means you now have lots of people doing things the wrong way. So the process of deciding who should help you train is critical. Also, I can't begin to describe how motivational this is for the chosen employee. Not only is he motivated to help with the training but also it inspires him to continue performing at peak levels. This is natural. If someone is sharing the secrets to success, he will naturally be reminding himself of what to do and how to do it. And he would never want the trainees to see his own performance slip so he will naturally continue to keep up his own productivity.

Think about all the ways that you and your company will win here. You get some help while you're creating additional motivation in a current employee who is helping new hires get a positive start. And this will result in more successful employees who will stay longer and be more productive for you and the company. Meanwhile, that helpful employee is more motivated and more driven to succeed. And this creates a desire in the other employees for the same opportunity. Does this sound like a pretty solid situation? On a scale of 1-10 it's about a 12! And you don't have to limit this to closing skills. You can do the same thing with answering objections and other sales skills that are relevant to the success of your particular call function.

You've already read Chapter 4 so you know the importance of ongoing training. When giving employees additional responsibility here, you can pump up the same amount of motivation as you can with the initial training. In fact, the two are almost exactly the same. I like to begin some days or meetings with group announcements. And sometimes I include what I call a *training brief* and I exercise this formula of *extra responsibility = non-monetary motivation*. Again, decide on who deserves it; talk with him (her) about what you would like him to accomplish, exactly what his role is, and then put it into action. I have used famous quotes, telephone tips, sales ideas, and motivational phrases for these morning training briefs. Never, ever have I been unable to identify one of my employees as a perfect fit to help with this form of training. And while I have had a few people decline out of fear of public speaking, most have jumped at the chance to be up on stage delivering their spin on how to be successful. And don't feel that you lost out if people decline. Even though they refused, they are still motivated by the fact that you thought of them and asked them. I have also seen some people get over their fear and take me up on a future role.

Brown bag training luncheons (Chapter 4) present another fine opportunity to have employees help you train other employees. Your preparation will be the same as before. Determine the employee you would like to take the additional responsibility, share the importance of the training session, set the date and then just sit back and watch the motivation take over. One of the perks about this form of non-monetary motivation is that it doesn't take place only during the activity. It begins right after you tell them, continues during their preparation time, goes on during the event and lasts for a long time after.

The above examples represent a few training ideas that you can put into action immediately. And I hope others come to mind according to how your training programs are structured. This is such a natural way to motivate some of your people and it requires no cash. And the end result is that everyone wins—the deserving employee, the employees they trained, you, and most importantly, your company.

## SCRIPTWRITING

While this opportunity may not surface too often, it does represent a fine opportunity to delegate additional responsibility as a form of non-monetary motivation. Whenever I am writing new scripts and call guides or revamping the old ones, I like to include a deserving member of the staff even if other managers and supervisors are involved—in fact, especially if other managers and supervisors are involved. This makes the employee feel all that much more special and appreciated. And the more special and appreciated he feels, the more motivated he will be. And don't think of this only as an opportunity to squeeze in some additional responsibility for someone. Why wouldn't you want help from some of your best people, the people who are going to be using the script? The people who deal with the script everyday and know where they are getting stopped and turned down or what section seems to help them sell the most? Go through your normal routine to determine the deserving employee(s) and get them involved from the beginning. Let them know that you are going through the critical task of writing new scripts or changing the current ones, that their help is needed and appreciated and that they are deserving. When making changes to current scripts, I always give them the task of taking the script home (or working on it during break time or lunch), making the changes they feel would be positive and then bringing their changes to our next meeting. Then everyone discusses it together and a new script is drawn up for trial use based on the meeting. If adjustments are necessary, make them accordingly. Whenever we are creating a new script or call guide, I give everyone the necessary information to drive the script and then go through the same procedures until the final script is developed. This may take several meetings since you are beginning from scratch. You can also use people in this area when developing responses to common objections. Once again, who could be better at helping you? Your people know what they're hearing every day better than you and I, so why count on the old crystal ball? Get them involved in the same way we described for script writing.

One thing is for sure, getting help from your employees on creating scripts and handling objections is not just an opportunity to trade some responsibility for some motivation. You're going to gain some serious benefit from this as well and so will the other employees. Your staff will be more positive about using a new script when they know that one of their own was involved in creating it. This always feels different than when it was created by the *power tower* and handed down to them. See the difference? And ultimately, as always, the company wins too.

## MEETINGS

Meetings? What meetings? If *meetings* sounds too vague, let's look a little deeper. I'm talking about giving certain deserving employees the extra responsibility of participating in selected meetings to give their input on any subject or issue at hand. Too often, meetings consist of only managers and senior level executives trying to figure out how certain issues, changes, or policies will effect your employees and their jobs. And this brings us to another question. Why not include one or more of them and get some real insight, ideas and solutions? I have two types of meetings where I have found it valuable to invite employee input and, at the same time, gain a lot of motivational mileage.

**Planning sessions**. Do you ever hold these? If not then do *plan* on having a planning session! If your answer is yes, I'm proud of you. Personally, I can't imagine not having small planning sessions throughout the year. You should at least hold one large planning session as you prepare for each upcoming year. I usually hold the annual one offsite at a local hotel. If you have a relationship with any specific hotel, ask them for a complimentary suite or conference room for the day. I've been able to get a freebie about 75 percent of the time, as long the hotel can spare the space on that day. And in other cases I have been able to get a most reasonable rate. Just put on your sales cap and ask!

This day-long session that plans the upcoming year covers everything from employee changes to motivational ideas, from the necessary adjustments regarding departmental policies to corporate suggestions and solutions. While the meeting is usually limited to my management team and administrative assistants, I always include one or two salespeople for their views on certain subjects. I set up a certain time for them to arrive and at that time we discuss the issues that they are there to discuss. We still have the management privacy we need for most of the day but we've generated high levels of motivation by briefly including some staff level employees. This session is always planned ahead so the chosen employees are notified well ahead of time as to the subject matter on which we'd like their input. Yes, it means additional responsibility, additional time and additional work. Do they mind? Hardly! Being asked to participate in the annual planning session is considered *big time*. And guess what? During the ten years or so that I have done this, some of the best ideas, most sensible solutions and overall solid input has come from these highly motivated employees.

**Meetings on policy changes.** Whenever policy changes are in the air and meetings are scheduled for deciding the changes, don't leave out one of the most important elements, the input from your employees. Now don't get me wrong, I'm not at all suggesting that you allow your employees to dictate what the divisional or corporate policies should be. What I am saying is that one of the angles we always look at is the way it will impact the staff. I hope this is always part of the discussion, it certainly should be. Why is it that we as managers and supervisors think we can envision all the results before we make a change? We may think we know and might even have a pretty accurate idea as to how people will react, but doesn't it make sense to just get some employee input to confirm how it will really be perceived? The answer is absolutely yes, as long as it's from the right people. Be careful here as you select one or more individuals for this responsibility. Be sure to choose strong, mature employees capable of giving you solid input, not complainers who won't be able to visualize the big picture.

This doesn't mean that every meeting you have must include staff extras and for the whole meeting. We're just suggesting that you be sensitive to including them in the portions of those meetings that discuss certain issues. But be careful here. Don't pull people in during a meeting for their input and then shove them out to get back on the phone. To make this successful, the employees should feel like a real part of the meeting and the issues at hand, and rightfully so. While it can be appropriate to spontaneously invite someone when you're in need, try to give the employees advance notice about the meeting and the topic to allow them time to prepare.

Many times I have gained important insight that I might not have thought of without giving these people the responsibility of being involved. Again, while I'm not suggesting that policies and procedures be structured to make sure those employees approve, it will help you to appreciate their outlook and perhaps understand better how to implement the necessary changes for a smooth transition. I have always found that even if their ideas are not used in the final solutions, they always appreciate the opportunity to be heard. I have also found that they gain a better understanding of the necessary changes because they have listened to discussions that support both the company and the employee. The big advantage here is that they will also communicate this better understanding to the rest of the employees, which guarantees you a smoother transition. These are two specific examples that you can use right away. But don't limit yourself to these two. When you find new opportunities like these to include additional responsibility, you will also be finding opportunities to gain additional motivation.

## VISITOR GUIDE

This responsibility is always well received and presses the old motivation button in everyone who participates. Whenever your department has a visitor (a customer, a manager from another department, a client, etc.), select someone to help you or the person in charge of departmental tours. The helper can play whatever role you choose but it usually works best to have them *show and tell* something about the day-to-day call functions they are involved in. Their superiority in this area must be part of the reason you selected them in the first place, so it makes sense, doesn't it? This was a hard one for me to let go of, but I'm so glad I did. I always thought I was the only one who should be doing the tours and I had the ego malfunction of thinking I could do it better than anyone else could. While there may be some specific tours that only you should give, there are some that will go quite well with the help of your deserving employees. Did you ever have this chance? I never did, but always wanted it. Think about the motivation that gets ignited here, the feelings of importance that surface as this person is showing your visitors around your department and explaining how things work. Once again we're talking about that special motivation switch called pride. When selecting the deserving employee, be sure to look at the individual's communications skills and how he (she) present himself along with whatever success made you consider him. While someone's performance standards make him a deserving choice, he may not be the best person for this task for other reasons. Find someone deserving based on work ethics and performance as well as people and presentation skills.

The importance of social gatherings and divisional get-togethers will be laid out in detail in an upcoming chapter. For now, let's stick to the subjects at hand—additional responsibility, the resulting motivation and a way to tie it into social gatherings and company get-togethers. Very simply, delegate the responsibility of all the preparation to members of your staff. That's it, that's all and there ain't no more! Well, there's a little more, but just the details. But the concept is that simple and once again it works!

Whenever you hold a social gathering, company picnic or special get-together, take this opportunity to assign some additional responsibility and stimulate some motivation. Choose some of your more responsible employees to head up different committees for the event. Every summer I hold a divisional summer picnic whether there's an overall company picnic or not. I assign people to head up each area of responsibility. I have teams of two employees specifically assigned to the areas of food purchase, adult games, children's activities, food preparation and cleanup. They have separate meetings getting the volunteer list together to arrange what food everyone will bring, planning adult softball, volleyball and other competitions, children's games and activities by age groups, assigning the grilling and hot food preparation and putting together a clean-up team. Then I meet with each group a few times as the date approaches offering some minor suggestions while also applauding their efforts and dedication. I have never heard anyone utter a word of frustration regarding the extra responsibility. And in fact I have always been thanked for including them in the planning stages and letting them do it virtually on their own. Give me one good reason not to do it this way. I know, you can't. And that's my point. The event is being planned by the people and for the people. The planners appreciate the opportunity to be involved and lead the way for everyone. And ultimately you generate motivation with the event itself and especially in the employees who organize it.

Summer picnics are only one possibility. I've done this same thing for other events such as Christmas parties, spring flings at the beach, Thanksgiving celebrations, and putting up holiday decorations. Since planning these events involves a lot of work, I'm sure you can use the help and I know you'll appreciate the motivation that comes along with it. While some events and gatherings will have more categories and more planning than others will, every single one produces the same opportunity for you to capitalize on. I've never seen any of these examples turn out any other way than positive all around.

These five ideas are just examples of the many ways and occasions you can utilize this fine non-monetary motivator, *additional responsibility*. Perhaps you already do these and many more. Perhaps some of these ideas have generated other ideas. That's great. Now put them to use. Remember that knowledge doesn't help you if you don't use it. The application of knowledge is what makes it powerful.

Now you're read about the many fine results that come from delegating extra responsibility. But I've been saving the best for last. As you observe your people handling these small, added responsibilities, you are actually identifying potential for future leadership. That's right, while all this other positive stuff is happening, you're also indirectly finding out who may be your next promotion. Isn't life great? Think about it. Your employees are

taking on extra responsibility and they are feeling more motivated because they feel included. And you get to have a bird's-
eye view of their capabilities pertaining to future promotions.
We've seen a lot of win/win/win situations in this book, for the
employees, for you, and for the company. Well, this is the way
it should and can be. And now that you know how to use additional responsibility as a non-monetary motivational tool, you
can make this a reality.

# 13

# Outside Seminars

Since you're reading this book I'm assuming you hold a position that makes you a candidate for attending seminars and job-related presentations. Assuming you've been, didn't you find it a nice change of pace, getting to do something out of the ordinary for a few hours, a full day or more? Sure it is, and taking a stimulating break is only one good reason to attend, right? Obviously, seminars are also educational so they contribute toward the improvement of your job. Therefore they expand your knowledge, management ideas, capabilities and income potential, as well as your chances for promotion. And this in turn presents opportunities for further responsibilities and financial growth. Seminars also offer networking opportunities for sharing ideas, concerns and solutions with industry colleagues. In addition to all of these direct business benefits, the seminar provides social time where new personal and professional friendships and relationships are generated, adding yet another reason you to look forward to going, right? Right, I feel the same way. And if you put all of these reasons together into one word you could say *motivation*. Attending seminars is, has always been and will always be motivating to most employees. Knowing that, let's consider how seminars can be another important piece in our puzzle called *non-monetary motivation*.

We just established many of the reasons why seminars motivate us. Now consider that our employees have the same emotions and desires. In fact, these same needs are alive and kicking in most of our employees. Too often we're all guilty of taking things for granted and not realizing how important those same things might be to someone who is not used to having them. And seminars are a perfect example. We as executives, managers and supervisors may have the option to attend seminars at will or to at least budget for them and get approval accordingly. It's that simple and we rarely give it a second thought. If you've had this luxury in the past and then lost your option to attend seminars, conferences or conventions, didn't you miss it? I'd be surprised if you didn't say yes. I've been there, I know. For years I attended any and all seminars and conferences at my own choosing and I had the privilege of meeting many of you during my presentations at most of the national and international conventions. Then suddenly after accepting an executive role with a new company, I found out that educational seminars and conferences were not on their list of important budget items. And for the next five years I had to do without them as part of my professional life. Five years. Not only did I miss going to them but also I really appreciated their value.

My point at the beginning of this chapter was for us as professionals to establish the true value of seminars and the motivation they generate. And again, that same value, that same motivation based on the same reasons that we like going to them also applies to our employees.

Your people need training in addition to what they get from you. I hope that sentence didn't make you angry. Here's another chance for us to get off our ego horse and listen to reason. None of us knows it all, senses it all, or can present it all. Like it or not, no one person can cover everything. Therefore, our people can use some training from someone else in addition to us. Not only is that all right, it's healthy, stimulating and without question, motivational. Part of the reason is that the information is coming from someone different. We're with them all the time, training and offering them advice. But seminars present them with the opportunity to receive training from another source. And you probably know what happens. Many times they will hear information that we as their leaders have been trying to beat into them without much success. But somehow it makes a difference coming from someone else because suddenly it gets *received and believed.*

I know what your reaction is because it's the same as mine was. "How come they believe that from someone else when I've been telling them that forever?" I learned a long time ago that these words are spoken by the ego but we all hear them. We've all had the frustration of failing to get one or more employees to understand something. And then along comes John Q. Seminar leader who briefly touches on the same issue and—bingo, the light comes on, sirens go off, bells ring and the employee learns a fantastic tip for success. I know, I know, gasoline has just rained on your fire of frustration. I have suffered through the same feelings until someone made me look at it differently. You see I've been on both sides. While living the same operational life that you live as managers, I have been presenting seminars for local and national conferences and conventions and private companies for years. And this has given me a clear view from the other side. And then one day it was made so clear to me by a telemarketing supervisor during a consulting assignment. I felt a little bad when a supervisor approached me after my presentation to her sales reps on the art of answering objections. She said, "You know, I have been trying forever to get them to look at objections as buying signals for all the same reasons you just discussed and they haven't responded. They're going crazy back there in the break room talking about how good the presentation was and how they were going to use the ideas the minute they got back on the phones." I felt uncomfortable and awkward. I fidgeted with a few sentences to play down my effect on her employees and then she interrupted me with the following sentence that I will never forget. She said, "No, Dave, don't feel bad, I'm not upset, not at all. In fact, I'm glad, I'm excited! As long as they learn what I've been trying to show them and they are more successful because of it, then whatever it takes to make it sink in is fine." She was simply interested in the development of her sales staff and she didn't get caught up in the egotistical nightmare that her employees learned something from someone else that she couldn't get them to learn.

Let me share another experience to clarify this point. There were many times during my years of private consulting that the divisional or corporate leaders have requested that my presentation or training be strategically planned. They recognized that my touching on specific subjects would bring the response they've been looking for since they've already done their own training on those issues. Their plan was to have me solidify the information by strategically placing it somewhere in my presentation, knowing the employees will pick it up and use this "new" knowledge. In other words, it is healthy to give your people these training briefs and additional seminars. I have also learned something that turned on the light for me. Not only are my employees grateful to me for what they learn at seminars because I gave them a chance to go, but more importantly, the light would never have been switched on if I hadn't built the foundation first. All of your hard work has not been wasted. As you can see, the truth is just the opposite. It's probably due to the work you and I have done as their managers that gets them to the point where they actually hear the information from a seminar leader or consultant. I was just too blinded by my own ego to see this before. How's your eyesight?

**Yes, seminars are affordable.** Now, before you panic about the cost of national seminars and conferences, hear me out. While some of you may be in position to send your employees to the larger national conferences, most companies are not and that's okay. But all of you are in a position (or can put yourself

170

in position) to identify some less expensive, half-day or full-day seminars that are offered locally. And don't assume that these aren't affordable either. Not only are they affordable for anyone, the value your employees and your company will gain will far exceed your small initial investment. Corporations like CareerTrack (1-800-488-0935) offer tremendous half-day and daylong seminars for less than $150 per person, some less than $100! They offer a wide range of topics relevant to any job and some specific to telephone techniques, sales and other business by phone subjects. And these are offered all over the country. Call them for a list of seminar topics, pick out a few out, check out the closest location to you (some will be right in your hometown) and get ready for a profitable investment. In fact as investments go, you could consider this chapter *insider information*. I might as well be telling you about a sure-fire investment that pays motivational dividends and that yields more productive and profitable performance for you and your company.

If you're pondering the expense of sending a group or all of your people to seminars, I have the following two suggestions for you:

**1. Check into an onsite seminar** and compare it to the expense of sending many employees to an offsite presentation. It all depends on your needs and how many people you're sending. I often get hired to present in-house corporate seminars and I'm sure that many companies see this as a cost-effective opportunity for all of their employees to benefit from a presentation. I've also had speakers and presenters come to companies where I have worked to perform in-house seminars. While these are usually considered in environments with large numbers of employees I have also done many for companies with only five to twenty telemarketing employees. The reasons for going in-house are simple. First of all, to have someone come in-house means that no travel is required by any employees which in turn means less time away from the phone and their regular daily responsibilities. It also means that travel expenses will be limited to one person, the presenter. But most importantly, it means that every employee is exposed to the seminar content, not just one person or a few people. Everyone hears the same thing, and more importantly, everyone is exposed to the energy and excitement of a live presentation. Everyone benefits from the questions and answers and the peak level of employee interaction.

Often during my in-house seminar presentations, employees from other departments have also been included when the subject matter focuses on generic issues such as positive attitude, listening skills or any other subjects that might benefit an employee in any department. And that should alert you to a positive factor in your consideration of an in-house seminar. Always ask yourself if anyone from other departments such as customer service, collections or other telephone departments could benefit from the in-house seminar you are considering.

**2. Make anyone who attends an outside seminar your *in-house trainer* for a day.** Whenever you send someone to an offsite seminar, make him or her responsible for feedback training to the other employees when they return. In other words, they will bring back the guts of the seminar and present it to the entire team at a scheduled time. I always help them glean the highlights and explain to them how I would like it presented. There are some real advantages to doing this both educationally and motivationally. Let's consider them now.

**Attention Span.** When someone knows he will assume the role of trainer upon his return, you have just been assured that his attention at the seminar will be in sharp focus. Wouldn't yours? I have been in this position and I promise you this hap-

172

pened to me. I remember the feeling when I learned that I would deliver a brief training session on the highlights of the seminar I was attending. The feeling was a mixture of anxiety, excitement and pride. And yes, there was also a feeling that I better pay close attention to every word, every slide, every overhead and every molecule of material at the seminar. And of course, I did. I gave a one-hour lunchtime presentation of the seminar highlights to all the other employees. It was one of the proudest moments of my early telemarketing career.

As a leader, you win in a couple of ways here. First of all, your employee will naturally learn more at the seminar by paying closer attention. And the other employees will learn from the post seminar training. And secondly, you have just generated a lot of motivation within your environment. The employee going to the seminar is motivated and other employees will now be further motivated for a chance to go to a future seminar and be the *trainer for a day.*

**Training leader.** As we just mentioned, there's some real motivational impact on most people when they get to be a leader in front of other people, especially their own co-workers. The opportunity to educate the entire staff about seminar information is stimulating to say the least. And therefore, the individual going to the seminar will take an active role in digesting as much information as possible knowing he or she will be presenting the highlights to the others. And presenting these highlights to the others is when the real advantage comes in, making this a cost-effective system. By sending one person to a seminar, you can educate your whole team, *as long as you send the right person.* Make sure you send someone that can and will present a brief and coherent synopsis of the seminar highlights.

Another way to get maximum motivation from seminars is to have employees earn the right to go. They can each select a seminar, compute the overall cost and turn it into a contest prize. Be sure to set your contest guidelines to represent coverage for whatever portion of the cost you deem necessary. When any employees reach your elevated performance standards (you determine the number), they earn the right to go to the seminar. This can range from one person to the first three or five, to anyone and everyone who reaches it. Remember that if you set the guidelines correctly, they're actually paying their own way. And they're going to be further educated and motivated by the opportunity to go. You will win all the way around. Local, inexpensive seminars offer the perfect opportunity to use this option.

I have found over the years that people are motivated by seminars as a contest prize. Keep your eyes and ears open for local seminars and business presentations that will help the personal and professional growth of your employees and reward them with attendance. By the way, pat yourself on the back because when you reward them with seminars you are rewarding yourself and your company. Good job!

**To summarize,** seminars should be part of your training structure and will provide a variety of ways to motivate your people. Look for cost-effective outside seminars and then utilize that person as *trainer for a day* to educate the other employees. Whenever possible and the budget allows, schedule an onsite, in-house seminar for group stimulation and education. And remember; don't block your employees' development by not letting them learn from anyone other than yourself. This hurts your employees, yourself and your company. Seminars are stimulating and motivational because they provide education. Education means learning, learning means getting better, getting better means happier and more productive. Happier and more productive means more success, more success means greater pride and higher income and all of the above equals a better chance of long-term, profitable employees.

# 14

# Casual Dress Days

I f you're looking for a novel way to offer some non-monetary motivation that doesn't require you to do anything, here you go. *Casual dress days* have more motivational impact in the formal corporate environments than in the more casual business-to-consumer telemarketing arena. And of course, the impact will vary in environments that fall in between these two extremes. But don't you dare stop reading this chapter just because you work in a casual environment. You'll find some original ideas that will bring some variety even where casual dress is the daily norm, so hang in and read on.

At the other end of the spectrum where conservative business attire (dresses, jackets and ties, etc.) are required, casual dress days are most certainly appreciated because they are novel, rare and stimulating. If this describes your environment, you know that formal business clothes can get pretty tiring, can't they? Guys, you know the starched, button-down dress shirt routine, fooling around until you get the tie knotted correctly, making sure the shoes are lookin' good, and finding socks to match. And ladies, you probably have to get up a little earlier too, to dress professionally for work.

While these examples describe the two extremes, many of your environments probably lie somewhere in the middle, which means that the resulting motivation lies somewhere in the middle. And if you've had it driven into your head that casual days are not good because they produce a casual effort, allow me to play brain surgeon and surgically remove that thought process from your head. If this has actually been your experience then I must tell you it's a management issue and not a fashion problem. I went through this phase years ago and finally realized that if production was down on casual days, it certainly wasn't because people were wearing jeans and a Polo shirt. It was the same problem as any other down day, a management issue. I started going the preventive maintenance route and letting everyone know that if casual days were not as productive as they needed to be, we simply wouldn't have them anymore. Since most people really appreciate them, they always make sure that casual days are productive days and in many cases they work harder to ensure it.  In fact, I know of some billion-dollar corporations that have adopted an *always-casual* dress code. That's right, five days a week, including executive staff. Do you think this would happen if casual days produced casual effort? Would these highly successful corporations implement policies to decrease sales and profitability? What do you think?

Even in the *always-casual* environment, some of the following ways to use casual dress days as employee motivation will still be effective. And even though I have used every one of these ideas, some may not be possible in your department. Others are feasible but remember that sometimes you have to fight for what you want and then prove that it's positive. If you ever run into executive opposition put on your sales cap and go for what you believe in. Here are some ideas that I know will work.

### 1. HOLIDAYS

Holidays are the perfect opportunity for a casual dress day throughout the year. If your company is closed on the actual holiday, use the closest preceding workday for the casual day. You can increase the holiday spirit by adding *Color Day* according to the holiday. Encourage people to wear red and green for

Christmas, red, white and blue for July 4th, black and orange for Halloween, red and pink for Valentines Day, and so on. Not all of the holidays will lend themselves to *Color Day* but they all present an opportunity for at least a casual day. *Color Days* are a good idea for those companies that are always casual. This adds a new twist to the ordinary casual, which makes it different and therefore motivational. Whenever there's business as usual on a holiday, have the casual or color day on the actual holiday.

## 2. THEME DAYS

In the chapter on theme contests we suggested having the employees dress according to theme. While contests sometimes coincide with these casual days, it's certainly not a requirement. Here are some themes I have used many times in different environments.

**Bright Color Day.** Have all your people wear the brightest thing hanging in their closets. They may also want to wear their shades because with an office full of oranges, yellows, fuchsias, chartreuse and neon colors, it gets pretty bright. It also gets pretty lively and therefore pretty productive.

**50s/60s Day.** Everyone seems to relate to this nostalgic era so jump on it. I sometimes have a 50s day separate from 60s day and other times I combine the two eras into one casual day. Whichever way you go, it will inspire penny loafers, white socks, pegged jeans and white T-shirts, poodle skirts, saddle shoes or Keds, madras shirts, Converse tennis shoes, bell-bottom jeans and tie-dyed T-shirts. And in some cases, leisure suits sneak in there. Although these suits weren't popularized until the 70s, I have always had one or two people show up in these polyester beauties. If you have the option to play music in your department, be sure to surf the dial for your local oldies

177

channel or spin your own stacks of wax like I do. Bring in cassette tapes, CDs or even an old turntable, take some dedications and be DJ for a day. I run this casual day at least once a year and usually more because it's such a favorite.

**Hat Day.** Invite your employees to wear their favorite *headwear*. You'll see everything from favorite sports team caps to cowboy hats, from bonnets to top hats, from straw hats to Hawaiian specials and plenty of unidentified varieties.

**Western Day.** No, this event is not limited to Texas or the western states. Regardless of what city or state I've been in, this has always been one of the most popular theme casual days since everyone likes wearing jeans. But it doesn't stop there. Some will be decked from head to toe with western style hat, bandanas, jean shirt or jacket, jeans, western belt, cowboy boots and sometimes spurs and chaps. I always have at least one guy going for the J.R. Ewing look. And while they can't dress as sharp as old J.R., I've seen some pretty fancy duds. I have also taken this perfect opportunity to grill hot dogs in the parking lot at lunchtime. The people who reach certain productivity levels in the morning get some free grub rustled up by me. This one's a no-brainer, folks, so jump on it.

**Formal Day.** Here's a chance for your employees to dress in their fanciest threads. Everyone likes to dress up every now and then and this gives them all the chance to do it in front of their peers. You'll see everything from tuxedos with tails and formal gowns to Sunday church clothes. This theme is a big hit in everyday casual environments because it works in reverse. Just as much as a casual day is motivational in a professional dress environment, a *Formal Day* motivates people in a casual atmosphere.

**Tropical Day.** I hold this casual day in warm weather so people will be comfortable in their Hawaiian shirts and sandals. Some fine hats will surface here and many people wear leis around their necks. Sometimes I get out some of my favorite music and crank up the old Beach Boys or Jan and Dean. And for the Elvis fans, I always play his version of the Hawaiian Wedding Song and other favorites from the *Blue Hawaii* album.

These theme days are always a hit and I'm sure you can come up with many more ideas that work equally well. Theme days are different, they're fun and they're effective.

## 3. BIRTHDAYS/PRE-VACATION DAYS

These two occasions present individual opportunities for casual dress days that are motivational because they are different than other theme days. These events are just for an individual who is celebrating his (her) birthday or the last day of work before he goes on vacation. It recognizes the day and it focuses on those particular people all day. It makes them special and therefore motivated. My employees flaunt their special casual day, reminding everyone throughout the day of exactly what day it is.

## 4. SPORTS RECOGNITION

Sports themes have endless possibilities. I always use this opportunity during the major sporting events such as the World Series, Super Bowl and NBA finals to have people dress in the colors of their favorite team. They also wear assorted team paraphernalia such as jerseys, buttons and caps.

As we discussed in the chapter on theme contests, this is also effective during big time local rivalries. When I worked in Alabama, I always held a casual dress day prior to the Alabama vs. Auburn football game. And while most people dressed in their crimson red, there were always some in their Auburn blue and orange. The mood is already primed for the big game so that sets the tone for employees to sport their team colors. This is also an opportune time for a team contest but either way this casual day will be effective.

## 5. SPONTANEOUS

Every now and then I announce a casual day . . . *just because*. No special reason, *just because*. These spontaneous casual days are sometimes the most popular ones because there are unexpected. Isn't it fun to get surprised with good news? Casual days are no different. They require no planning; you simply announce them the day before. Like other special days, don't announce these too often or they'll no longer be a surprise and they'll lose their sense of fun.

## 6. SPECIAL ACHIEVEMENTS

I have also used special performance standards or record-breaking as a reason to announce a casual day. Sometimes when a divisional performance record is set or a calling project is completed, I may call a casual day for the next workday. This can be done by separate teams or for the entire department.

## 7. CONTEST PRIZE

Casual days are such an effortless way to reward people. And don't confuse effortless with less effective. I started using this in the 1980s and because they're so valuable I've never stopped. Again, the effectiveness will depend on your current dress code. This is not really an option in casual environments. But when your dress week includes only one casual day, it's a big hit. Employees appreciate this so much they often request it as a prize. Also it offers a lot of flexibility. I have run daily contests where anyone reaching a specific percentage of their daily quota can dress casually the following day, so only those that earn it the previous day get to enjoy it. I have also rewarded contest-winning teams with a casual day for everyone on the winning team or the entire division (in the case of a divisional goal). I have also varied the number of days rewarded according to certain performance factors. Everyone who earns a casual day in the daily quota contest can earn another day by reaching a higher level above his quota. This keeps everyone working hard even after they have passed their goal. I have also rewarded contest-winning teams with a casual week for hitting aggressive goals during a contest. While they get one casual day for just being a member of the winning team they will push hard when a *casual week* is at stake. You can create all kinds of variations to use this fine motivator as a contest price.

Get busy and use these ideas to create some of your own to invite your people to dress up, down or a little wild and crazy. In many cases you'll find that it means more to your people than you would have guessed. And the best part is that it doesn't cost you a cent.

# 15

# Goodie Days
# (Pizza/Popcorn/Cookies)

Just what we need, another reason to eat, right? Exactly right. Every now and then a pizza, popcorn or cookie day breaks up the otherwise predictable routine and keeps people motivated. And there are many ways to use this enjoyable form of non-monetary motivation. First of all, let's consider what these goodie days are like and when you should offer them. A goodie day is any day that you choose for everyone to enjoy a pizza break, some popcorn or cookies provided by the employees. Sounds delicious, you're thinking, but why is this motivational? Goodie days offer a change, something out of the norm. Go back to your school days. I'll wait a minute here because if you're like me it takes a few minutes to remember that far back. Okay, ready? Remember the days that included a pep rally or field trip? On that day you were always a little more pumped up, right? It was something different that broke up the redundancy of the daily routine. Second, who doesn't like to eat goodies? Not too many people I know. Certainly not me! In fact, now that I think about it, I guess it's no surprise that I launched these eating bonanzas. Besides being a registered chocoholic, I'm probably qualified to organize a 12-step program called S.A. (Snackaholics Anonymous). We have a place in our kitchen that is affectionately known to our family and friends as the snack cabinet. Remember in the old cartoons when someone would open the kitchen cabinet or bedroom closet and an exaggerated quantity of stuff would pour out and cover the person who opened it? Well, that's not far from the truth when you open our snack cabinet. And while our cabinet is probably a lot fuller than yours is, the point remains that most people enjoy goodies. So why not feed the desire and the motivation at the same time? Following are a few ideas that have worked well in my environments and are certain to work in yours. There may be people who choose not to participate on any given day and that's to be expected. Force-feeding would defeat the purpose.

### 1. COOKIE EXTRAVAGANZA DAY

Invite everyone in your department to bring in a couple of dozen cookies of their choice on a given day (I usually pick a Friday) so that everyone can enjoy different types of cookies throughout the day. In addition to enjoying the different tastes many people trade recipes, which adds to the sense of camaraderie. While some employees bring store-bought cookies most will take the time to bake, which adds variety to the predictable Oreo's and Chips Ahoy. I try to hold a Cookie Extravaganza Day once a month or at least once a quarter, depending upon how many other special days we're recognizing.

### 2. DESSERT DAY

Obviously, Dessert Day is one culinary level beyond Cookie Day. In addition to cookies, you'll think you're in Sugar Heaven with cakes, pies, cheesecakes, sweet rolls and homemade candy. You'll find some people making more phone calls with more enthusiasm than usual. Dessert day, even more than cookie day, promotes the exchange of recipes along with the verbal approval and compliments between employees, which further builds a healthy environment. Desert day has always been a favorite. To quote the famous cereal ad, "Try it, you'll like it."

### 3. PIZZA PARTY DAY

Pizza is practically a registered party food that everyone

seems to enjoy. Have your company provide a pizza party for lunch, supper or during a short work break. If you're concerned about the expense, you can usually get impressive "two for one" deals at Little Caesars, or you can try working out a special price arrangement with a pizza place based on volume purchased. I have always found most pizza establishments to be more than generous when it comes to negotiating a deal. And depending on your company's line of business, you might even be able to negotiate a product trade for pizza. Find out what toppings everyone likes and order a nice variety. And if you can't get it delivered make sure you send someone to pick up the pizza early. Whether you serve it during a fifteen-minute break, over lunch or after work, pizza is always a nice break from the norm, which makes it an effective motivator.

### 4. POPCORN (and a movie)

If you're going to serve popcorn as a special treat, why not serve it in the setting where people enjoy it most . . . at the movies. No, I haven't lost my mind or joined a cult. I did say at the movies. Here's how you do it. Use one of the following opportunities:

**Break Time Movierama.** Pick out a favorite movie that suits most ages and both genders and schedule it for showing in segments over four to five days. Combine both the morning break with the afternoon break for anyone who wants to participate and you can now show 30 minutes of the movie each day during your now extended afternoon break. Now you can't go to the movies without getting popcorn right? I mean, it's practically the law. Each day prior to movie time makes sure there's plenty of popcorn. And don't go through the long task of making it yourself in the microwave or using the old Jiffy Pop method. Make it easy on yourself. Call your local movie theater, speak with the manager and purchase one of those huge bags of popcorn they make when they pop it there. You can also buy these large bags of popcorn at any candy and sweet store at your nearest mall. But the advantage of getting it from the movie theater is that you can usually get them to donate the individual popcorn containers so everyone can have their own. This adds to the fun and resulting motivation because it makes the environment more authentic. Prepare the conference room (or wherever you're showing it) for that time slot each day and have fun!

A crowd-pleasing variation of this event is to show famous episodes of old TV shows like *Andy Griffith* or the old *Our Gang* series. Remember the *Little Rascals* with Spanky, Buckwheat and the gang? Weren't those the greatest? Remember the time when they wrote the notes to get out of school and then found out the ice cream truck was coming to the school the next day so they broke into the school that night to take back the notes? And remember how big Stymie's eyes got when the hand of the skeleton dropped on his shoulder in the science room? And who can forget the *He-Man Woman-Haters Club* that Spanky and Alfalfa put together? Sorry about that, I got carried away. Just thinking about those old films makes me laugh, but let's get back on track here. This activity has always been a hit because almost everyone enjoys those shows. And when you fast-forward through the commercials each episode is only about 15-20 minutes long. You can usually watch two or three episodes of *Little Rascals* in less than thirty minutes. Get your popcorn, enjoy some laughs, and reap the big motivation that is certain to result.

**Movie Time After Hours.** Take a Friday, set up the movie for right after work and show it from beginning to end for everyone who wants to attend. Go through the same exercise for providing popcorn and simply enjoy the time together!

Popcorn days can also be celebrated without movies by serving large bowls of assorted popcorn for people to enjoy during their breaks. Pick up those large cans of popcorn that usually include caramel-covered, cheese-covered and regular. Popcorn is a festive snack your people will truly enjoy.

If you supervise a large telemarketing office or division, you're probably thinking that this event wouldn't be feasible. Larger environments are usually broken into teams with team leaders or supervisors for every 12-15 people. If so, you can show movies for different teams at different times. Keep in mind that not everybody will participate and that's all right. I'm certainly not pretending to know the size of all different telemarketing operations and how breaks are structured. My crystal ball is in the shop so I can't possibly know all the variables you're working with. What I don't need a crystal ball to tell you is that if you offer *movierama* with popcorn in your environment three or four times a year it works beautifully. The key word here is *works*, meaning it provides creative stimulation.

### 5. COOKOUT DAY

Another special food day that always scores motivational points is *Cookout Day*. Once or twice a year I set up a couple of gas grills in the parking lot in the morning and grill hot dogs for lunch. Serve them with potato chips, pickles and cookies and charge your employees one dollar per plate to offset your cost. Most everyone will participate and it creates a chance for people to relax and spend time with each other over the lunch hour. And here are two tips for added success.

**You should be the cook**. That's right, you! Grab the old white apron and a chef's hat and get out there. You should be the cook providing wieners off the grill. It not only shows your dedication to being involved but it also becomes a perfect time for you to share a little conversation with your employees as they assemble their lunches and wait for the hot dogs.

**Use this day to run a lunchtime contest.** Set goals of

60-70% of your employees' daily quota and offer a free lunch plate to any employee who reaches the goal. You'll naturally see an increase in morning productivity and everyone always enjoys the cookout. It all adds up to an enjoyable and successful day. And since there is a natural tendency for people to get excited in anticipation of something different, structure some of these cookout days in advance. If you give people notice they can look forward to it and have time to prepare whatever dish they might bring.

In addition, I sometimes surprise my employees by walking around with a large bowl of miniature Hershey chocolate bars, letting everyone take a few to enjoy a little midday energy boost. (If you do this, and I encourage you to, you might as well figure out something to do with all the leftover dark chocolate ones. Why is it that no one likes those? It's so funny; those are always the only ones left.) Another surprise treat is doughnuts. And for the summer I recommend Popsicle's and ice cream bars. Since most people like surprises *and* sweets, you can't really go wrong here.

I encourage you to try any and all of the ideas in this chapter. These goodies and treats are the simple ingredients that are part of the magic formula to help your people enjoy their workplace, which will always motivate them in their work.

# 16

# Team Spirit

I know what you're thinking. "Oh no, it's that overused word—as in team player or teamwork or teammate." Well, yes, it's one in the same. While the word team may be overused in the business world, the concept that it represents is usually underused, at least in our industry. "Pardon me, Dave," you ask. "Underused or not, how can team spirit be motivational?" Well, grab some coffee or a Coke, relax and read on. I think you'll find your question answered as well as some ideas that you can use immediately in your environment.

While it has always been important to be team-oriented at any level of business, this is a choice that individual employees make for themselves. If you want your employees to be team players—and you should—now consider this. Why they would *choose* to think of themselves as part of a team? And can you influence their choice?

Let's consider the second question first. You can definitely make a difference in your employees' choice about being team players. As the department leader, you can influence this decision more than anyone can. How? Simply by creating team spirit. When you create an atmosphere in your environment that eats, drinks, sleeps, breathes and lives teamwork, your employees will be much more likely to choose the team player attitude over the solo mentality.

Let's dissect the idea of team player for a minute and make sure we're on the same page. What does it mean to be a team player? Well, the best way to answer that is to think about two people you know, one who's a devoted team player and another who flies solo. I'll give you about five seconds to come up with both. Okay, I know you've already got them pictured. First let's look at the person you thought of who probably can't even spell *team*. He (or she) is probably like the person I have in mind:

- He doesn't interact positively with other employees;
- He doesn't think too much about divisional or corporate goals, only his own goals;
- He doesn't offer help or assistance very often with department or divisional activities or projects;
- He seldom attends group outings, social gatherings, or company get-togethers;
- He seldom shows concern for long-term planning or the big picture, only concern for himself;
- In social conversations where work is discussed, he is often critical of your company, executive leaders, products or other employees;
- During theme contests, he doesn't display any team inclination or enthusiasm and is only consumed by his own performance or what he will personally win.

I'm sure there are other dysfunctional qualities we've omitted here. And I'll bet if you didn't have someone in mind earlier, you do now—maybe several people. To put it bluntly, these people just don't get it. Maybe the problem is stubbornness, selfishness, or a desire to resist conformity. Maybe it's a combination of these with a few extras thrown in.

Now think about your ultimate *team* player that's just the opposite. Do you know this person?

- He (she) interacts positively with other employees;
- He understands that while individual goals are important, everyone wins when you achieve corporate goals;
- He often offers help with department or divisional projects;

- He participates in group outings, company get-togethers and social gatherings as often as possible;
- He is constantly trying to understand the big picture and how he fits into it;
- He is supportive of the company, co-workers, executive leaders, products and services in conversations about work;
- During team contests he encourages teammates and looks at team totals first and individual achievements second.

Oh, you know this employee? Yeah, me too. Again, if you hadn't thought of this person earlier I'm sure someone comes to mind now. Maybe you know someone whose picture would appear in the dictionary under *team player*. And as much as the non-team players don't get it, these people do get it. They understand that when you put your division and company goals first, the individual goals will often be achieved as well. It's a simple concept; when the team wins, everyone wins, and if the team loses, no one wins.

Consider the activity of sports, where teamwork is most evident. The hockey player glides down the ice toward a score only to dish off the puck at the last second to a teammate coming in from the side who then scores. A basketball player passes the ball instead of taking the shot, and then provides a screen for his (her) teammate to go around for the potential score. The baseball player swings wildly at a terrible pitch to protect his teammate who is trying to steal second base. The football player throws his body into an opposing player and provides the block that frees the ball carrier for a touchdown. The volleyball player sees an opening for her own shot but sets up her teammate for a spike to make sure the team gets a point.

The examples are endless but I think you get the picture. Team players see that proverbial big picture above their own single accomplishments. And while some people are team players by nature, most people get swept up in whatever attitude prevails in their workplace. And you as the department, division or company leader are more responsible for that attitude than anyone else. In sports, whenever you see players using team play, there is a good chance that the coaches and team leaders have created a team spirit within the clubhouse, the organization and most importantly in the minds of the players. It's your responsibility to create the same feelings in your work environment and in the minds of your employees. Remember that team stands for **T**ogether **E**veryone **A**chieves **M**ore— together, with each other, for each other and for the overall benefit of the whole. Have we now established that team players are the employees of choice? In case you're not convinced, let's look at one more piece of this puzzle.

Most people like to belong, to be part of something rather than being alone. Most people have the desire to be part of the team, to have that good feeling of contributing to the overall success of group activity. So don't suppress this natural feeling. Expose it. Exploit it. Give your employees what they want, which is also what you want. Encourage them to be part of a team of employees who strive for overall departmental success and focus on the big picture together. Encourage them to look for ways to strengthen their environment through personal improvement and by helping each other however they can.

Now let's move on and explore how we, as leaders, can use this important element of team spirit to create and maintain a more motivational environment. And we did just spell motivation over the first few pages of this chapter, didn't we? An employee who is a team player and part of a spirited, successful environment is a happier, more productive employee. As I said, we just spelled *MOTIVATION*, and in capital letters. Now here are some ways to create team spirit and more importantly, to maintain it.

191

## 1. POSTERS/BANNERS

Posters and banners are continuous visual aids. Posters are easy to find or make, they're fairly inexpensive and they last for a long time. I go to my local teacher supply store and have fun choosing posters that illustrate the team concept. I have posters that picture team activities from tug-of-war to building a project together, with captions like TEAM . . . Total **E**nthusiasm by **A**ll **M**embers or **T**otal **E**ffort by **A**ll **M**embers (and the one we mentioned earlier, **T**ogether **E**veryone **A**chieves **M**ore). I post these throughout the work area, break rooms, on the entrance and exit doors, near the time clock and everywhere the employees will see them. I surround my employees with visible reminders of teamwork. Teacher supply stores are certainly not the only resource for posters. Successories (1-800-535-2773) has all kinds of teamwork paraphernalia like posters and cards. And their catalogs are awesome. I am never without my thick gold pocket coin from Successories that reads "Winning With Teamwork."

If your budget has suddenly gone south get creative and make your own banners. Use a computer program that looks good and you'll get the message across. Put up a nice mixture of purchased and homemade posters and banners. Another option is to get your employees involved. One way that has always worked well is making this a weekly or monthly team phrase responsibility. I put up a big corkboard (or just use the wall when there's no corkboard and the budget is low) and make a list of all divisional employees. And every week or month the employees alternate the responsibility of creating a team phrase. Whenever their names come up, they are responsible for a phrase or quote that highlights the word and meaning of team. They bring it in on Monday (or the first workday of the month), share it with the team, sign it and put it up on the wall or the corkboard. And if practical, leave all of them up for as long as possible. This will build a collage of team-oriented quotes and phrases as a tribute to your employees. This will also inspire motivation in two ways. First, you can't help but feel motivated when you sign your phrase or quote and put it up on the wall or board for everyone else to see. Second, just reading these whenever you pass by creates ongoing stimulation. Believe me, it works. My employees have brought in everything from "There is no 'I' in TEAM to "Less me and more we." They bring quotes from famous journalists, celebrities, sports stars and politicians as well as some they themselves make up. And while this exercise presents an extra responsibility, each person's name comes up infrequently. Many of your people will actually look forward to this. Sometimes my employees trade up for their turn because they came up with a good quote and don't want to wait until their name comes up. When they are involved in creating the team collage they will be stimulated whenever they see it.

These are just a few ideas that you can use in your environment. Use any one or combination and you will be putting another important piece into your motivational puzzle.

## 2. TEAM PICTURES

Most employees have the same reaction when a camera shows up in the department for a group photo. They sing the old "No, don't take my picture" song. They act like they would rather not have the picture taken or that they're camera shy. But when the camera gets aimed the tune changes. The smiles appear and everyone jockeys for a visible position. And if a picture gets taken before someone is ready, they beg for another chance. Why does the tune change so drastically? It's simple. Most people will *pretend* that they're embarrassed, shy and self-conscious about having their picture taken.

Now let's get down to the truth. Few people are really, truly camera shy. In fact, most people want to have their picture taken, which explains the last minute positioning for visibility. People want to be noticed in the picture, especially when

193

it recognizes a team for achievements and may be visibly displayed. Why? It's human nature to want to be noticed.

Team pictures give your employees the chance to be noticed and are therefore motivational. After getting the pictures developed be sure to put them up in a visible spot in your department. I always have a big corkboard for pictures. This also helps to enhance team spirit because every time people see the picture it brings on the feelings of belonging, of being on a team. What prompts a team picture, you ask? When should I take team pictures? The following ideas represent all the reasons I've used to take team pictures. Use these and any others you can think of to take an occasional group photo.

**Social Gatherings** • It is always healthy to use this off-site, off-time get-together for group pictures. These are usually fun and happy events and the pictures will reflect happy, smiling people enjoying themselves together. Holiday parties and company picnics also offer photo opportunities.

**Contest Winners** • If you ever break your people into teams for a contest, take a picture of the winning team(s) to hang up. This creates double stimulation because of (1) the association with winning and (2) simply having your picture displayed. If the contest has a specific significance or theme, take a team photo using an appropriate backdrop. Every now and then I will run a team contest based on percentage of quota. The following week we'll go to a local steakhouse like Ponderosa where the winners eat steak and extras while the losers eat beans—and serve the winners throughout the meal. I've always taken a team picture at the restaurant so that the full effect will be remembered for a long time. Whenever people look at these pictures they not only laugh, they have positive feelings about their team victory. And those who were not on the winning team are equally motivated to be sure they are in the next picture of winners.

**In-house Newsletter** • Remember the chapter on executive recognition when I told you about the big article that was written about my department? When this came out, I immediately clipped the team picture, attached it to an 8.5" x 11" sheet of copy paper, wrote something simple like, *"This team is awesome,"* and hung it up. This inspired instant and ongoing team spirit and motivation. If you ever have a group picture that gets published anywhere, do exactly what I did. I promise you, you'll get the same positive reaction and ongoing motivation that it provided in my department.

**Performance Record** • When a team or your department breaks a performance record for high standards of productivity, take a team picture and post it on your corkboard or wall. This is one of those double motivation pictures because it represents performance standards and that touches pride, and we all know what that does, right?

**Special Projects** • If a team completes a specific project within their goal dates, take their picture at the end, provided they do an excellent job on the project. This will also foster desires for future accomplishments and most of all, teamwork.

**Special Theme Contests/Days** • Theme contests or theme dress days are another photo opportunity. At least once a year I hold a *50s/60s Day*. Everyone dresses accordingly and we run a contest. This event always makes for great team pictures, showing employees in everything from poodle skirts and saddle shoes to tie-dyed T-shirts, flower power attire and peace jewelry. These type of pictures capture team spirit and are also just flat-out fun. I also take pictures on other theme dress days I have invented such as *Western Day, Brightest Color Day*, and *Favorite Hat Day*.

Theme contests based on big time sporting events also are

also team picture opportunities when everyone is wearing their team colors. I often hold a contest in April in honor of the Masters golf tournament. I divide people into teams of two or four players who must reach a specific productivity level for a chance to make a putt on a twelve-foot stretch of green indoor/outdoor carpet with a putter return device. One of my assistants dresses as a Masters caddy with full white overalls, white tennis shoes, green ball cap and a nametag on her back that reads "everyone." Some of the employees dress in golf attire and it makes a great team picture with our caddy and the putting green as a backdrop. Any time people are dressed in theme they love to have their picture taken, especially all together.

**Just Because** • It's that simple, just because. No special reason, no astronomical performance, no special theme day, not because they won a contest . . . simply spontaneous. On occasion, get everyone together (or by teams) for a picture and pin it up on your corkboard or wall. Many of these have become favorites and therefore some of the most effective when it comes to motivation.

At you develop your film and put up these team pictures you are developing team spirit and therefore developing a more motivational environment. NOTE: In order to capture the excitement of the moment, try using a Polaroid camera where the film pops out and develops right in front of you. But remember to also take photos with a standard camera because employees may want copies of the pictures. That's right, copies. And who was it that was camera shy in the first place? Yeah, right!

### 3. TEAM CONTESTS

While individual contests are just as effective in many cases, team contests will always stimulate those feelings of team spirit in your people. Whenever possible, I urge you to create team contests. Then watch the togetherness that evolves while they work together for a common goal. If your people are not organized into teams, this can be counterproductive if you're not careful about how you set up the teams. Be sure to balance the teams based on the capabilities of your people. Don't overload one team who will run away with the contest. And be sure to base the qualifications for winning on percentage of team quota. This ensures that all teams have an equal chance to win whether they have new people or seasoned veterans.

Whenever I run team contests that last longer than one day, I find it helpful to have the teams meet each day before the shift begins to discuss their game plan and get into the team spirit. Remember also that teams can be any size. A team can consist of just two people. I have run team contests that range from teams as small as two people to as big as the entire division representing one team.

## 4. MANAGEMENT EXAMPLE

Most leaders overuse the term *team player* as in "You can count on me to be a team player." But are you? Challenge yourself for a moment. I'm not challenging your integrity nor am I accusing you of not being a team player. But "I'm a team player" has become a canned phrase. Now I ask you one question. Do you *show* your employees that you're a team player? Do your employees see that quality in you? Remember that it's not what we say, it's what we do. Most people depend on the old Missouri "show me" attitude. Don't tell me; *show me*. This is natural. They want to *see* it in you. You are the ultimate creator and maintainer of team spirit—or not. Are you in some of those team pictures? If not, you should be. When you hold special theme dress days, do you dress up too? I do. When you set up the rotating responsibilities for "team theme" quotes and phrases, are you part of it? I hope so. If you don't set a good example for your people to follow you won't have much team spirit in your work area. It's as simple as that.

At my 1997 sales banquet celebrating the annual achievements and kick-off for 1998, I handed out cards (from my Successories catalog) to every employee in my division— sales people, administrative help, managers, everyone. The card said TEAMWORK in large letters, partially covering a picture of a group of people working together. Under the word TEAM-WORK, the caption reads, "Teamwork is the ability to work together toward a common vision, the ability to direct individual accomplishment toward organizational objectives. It is the fuel that allows common people to attain uncommon results."

I then held up my card and said that each one of them should think about what teamwork means to them and to write that inside the card and bring it back after the holidays. Then I read them what I had written in mine "There is nothing that can't be accomplished when the right people are caught up in a worthy cause." By doing this I showed them that I had already completed mine. After the holidays I took all their cards and copied the internal quotes, poems and phrases that everyone had submitted, made a collage and posted it in the work area. Then I had each person put their own card in their workstation where it was visible. Everyday they saw the word *teamwork* and what it meant to them. The key here is that I set the example. I filled mine out first and shared it with them. They knew I was committed to enhancing our team spirit and they followed me. I realize this is only one quick example. But you must be the leader and your employees must see and believe that you are the example to follow. How can you possibly expect them to get into the team spirit if you're not?

Get those posters and banners up, take advantage of opportunities for group and team pictures, structure some of your contests to involve teamwork and most all, set a positive example. If you do these things you will inspire team spirit in your environment, which will inspire your people, which will make them more motivated. And as we know, more motivated people are more productive, long-term employees. There is too much self-ishness and there are too many egotistical roadblocks keeping many departments, centers, and even companies from the satisfying results that teamwork and team spirit will bring to a work environment. Remember that there should be less "**I**" and "**me**" in your environment and more of "**us**" and "**we**."

# 17

# Stress Management

I f you're wondering how stress management and non-monetary motivation fit together, you're probably thinking about putting this chapter aside for another time, right? If I caught you, let me have your attention before you make a big mistake. Maybe you've heard those sayings like "anything can happen in the last inning," or "the caboose is the most important car on the train." In other words, this final chapter may not be the longest or it may not appear to be as useful for you. But these concluding pages are just as vital as the rest of this book for creating and maintaining a motivational environment. Just as the last scene of a TV show is crucial to the whole program, we don't want you to miss this finale. Stay tuned while we go to a quick commercial break and get ready to enjoy the final scene.

First, let's briefly consider the term *stress*. Webster defines stress as *tension or strain*. Now ask yourself, "Is there tension or strain in my employees?" If your answer is "not really," "not much," "I don't think so," or worse, "no," my sympathy goes out to you. I mean, I'm a compassionate guy so I feel bad for anyone who needs immediate counseling. If your answer is anything but an honest *yes*, you are grossly deceiving yourself and ultimately cheating your employees. Your staff needs you to understand that stress is very much alive and active in their work lives. Have you ever worked the phones prior to your management career? Can you remember the redundancy of call after call after call? Or the urgency of reaching your sales quota? Or the pressure of delivering your presentation in front (or at least within listening distance) of other people? If you were never on the phones before becoming a supervisor, picture yourself in your subordinates' role on an hour-to-hour, day-to-day basis. Could you do it? Would you want to? While I'm not diminishing the pressures that go along with our jobs as leaders, let's make sure we don't underestimate the stress that our employees experience and the effect it has on them.

**WHAT NOT TO DO . . . Do not ignore it.** Pretending that stress doesn't exist or that it's not a big issue is probably the worst thing you can do. We've already established that stress is there. If you brush it aside—or worse, ignore it, you might as well pour gas on a fire. And while you're performing that art, go ahead and write up some "help wanted" ads for the Sunday classifieds. You're going to need them. I made this mistake early in my career and have witnessed it hundreds of times with colleagues and in other companies where I've done consulting. Supervisors and managers in telemarketing take this subject lightly and it ends up costing them heavily. In most cases this issue can be addressed and for the most part, cured, before it reaches advanced stages. It almost sounds like a disease, doesn't it? Well, as I think about it, it does resemble a disease. You can prevent stress in some cases. Or you can diagnosis and deal with it in the early stages, and then continue with periodical checkups to make sure it doesn't flare up again.

**WHAT TO DO . . . Let's consider the kinds of resources you can offer your employees that will minimize stress and provide them with tools for dealing with it.**

### 1. Publications and tapes

There are many good books, articles and tapes about stress. For articles and books check with your local library, bookstores and the Internet. You'll find publications dealing with the full range—

partial prevention, how to identify stress and what you can do to handle and overcome it. Some materials will treat this topic more generically, but don't discount the value of general information about stress management. For corporate-specific information, you can check with the corporate offices of telemarketing magazines for past articles dealing with this subject. I have listed some suggestions at the end of this chapter

Though more expensive, audio and videotapes may be somewhat easier to find. Major bookstores are a good resource as well as companies and organizations that promote and distribute business-training materials such as CareerTrack Publications in Boulder, Colorado (800-334-1018). Local or national telemarketing conferences can also be a good resource for both audio and video taped materials. As you may remember in the chapter on training, I mentioned the importance of providing your department with a mini library of resources? Information on stress management is a resource that should definitely be in your library. And here are some other ideas:

- Encourage group audio or video sessions on stress management over brown bag lunches. This creates the opportunity for employee interaction, which adds to their awareness and education about this important subject.
- Stress management is a good subject for the self-improvement training sessions we talked about earlier. Since some of the programs on this subject include up to six audiotapes you can turn it into a series using a different tape each week.

Articles, publications and tapes on other subjects can also be helpful in your efforts to manage employee stress levels. Topics like a winning attitude, setting and achieving goals, positive self-esteem, personal and professional growth or any success-based focus can indirectly facilitate stress reduction. When people have more positive attitudes, when they're reaching their goals more often, when they have higher self-esteem and are progressing personally and/or professionally, corporate stress levels will naturally fall to a minimum. A good healthy mix of these available resources can serve as an antidote to the levels of stress that attack your work environment.

### 2. In-house seminars

A brief in-house seminar on stress management can be most effective. While professional speakers and presenters might be expensive, local physicians and university professors can provide valuable and less costly expertise. I have organized brown bag lunches (some mandatory and others voluntary) that included a 20- to 30-minute presentation on stress management by a knowledgeable doctor or teacher. Some charged a nominal fee while others have actually volunteered. It boils down to what you're willing to do as a leader and how important it is to see your employees succeed in a low-stress environment. And it's a test of how willing you are to do whatever it takes to find someone to speak to your team and organize the event. Preventative maintenance is a powerful means of reducing the chances of a breakdown later. I know so because I've lived it both ways. I've seen the difference. Stress management is something you can't afford not to do.

### 3. Flexible breaks and mealtimes

From experience, I encourage you to be as flexible as you can about break times throughout the work shift. Be as flexible as your business allows whether you're dealing with a part-time shift with one break or full-time shifts with two breaks and a lunch or dinner. If possible, try not to schedule breaks at fixed times. As managers, how do we know when our employees need to take a break? Some may need a breather just one hour into the morning while others like to wait until closer to lunchtime. We're dealing with individual preference, something that's important to the employee. Some people would rather wait than interrupt themselves while others may need time-out as soon as the first customer rearranges their brain. If people have the option of using their break when they need it, they will be happier and therefore less stressed.

Flexible breaks can be more difficult to keep track of if your staff is larger. You may be forced to set break times if you find this too difficult to control. You'll have to judge. If your employees take lunch and dinner breaks at scheduled times, try to be flexible when they request a different time based on personal needs. It's one of those little things that mean a lot. I've seen and been an employee in one of those *work prisons* with no flexibility and it was much too stressful. This is something that's usually easy to reorganize that can increase employee satisfaction—and therefore, motivation. Take a hard look at your setup and challenge yourself.

### 4. Other forms of non-monetary motivation

Here's the big one, the old granddaddy of 'em all, and the best way to create and maintain an almost stress-free environment. Notice I said *almost*. I've never seen or been in a totally stress-free environment so almost is about as good as it gets. If you've been sleeping through the rest of this chapter or scanning it for something to jump out at you, pay close attention because here is the secret. It's called *other non-monetary motivation*. That's right. The more items from the previous 16 chapters you use in your environment, the less stress management you'll need. This is not a theory. It's a fact. Think about it. If you put a solid compensation plan in place, if you give each of your people a title he can be proud of, if you provide good coaching and training that includes outside and inside seminars, if you offer some type of career path, if you recognize employee achievements, if you provide a healthy work environment energized by team spirit, if you create opportunities to earn time off and you set up a few family gatherings per year, if you create theme contests and have casual dress days, if you provide the chance for additional responsibility, if you throw in some pizza, popcorn and cookie days and are using some of the gimmick ideas for creative awards. . . then the stress that is all too evident in so many environments will be dramatically reduced in your division. If organizing these measures sounds like a massive amount of work on your part—rest assured that it is not. Start with a little at a time. Remember the old commercial for Brylcreme hair gel? Remember the jingle, *A little dab'll do ya*? Here too, a little dab of any combination of these non-monetary motivators *will do ya*. And employee stress will decrease. Implement a little dab of all of them in your department and see what happens. Go ahead and use your imagination. I already know what happens.

All of these ideas for stress management have worked for me and for others. They will also work for you, but only if you recognize that stress exists and it requires your attention. Be sure to keep your management eyes and ears open so you can look and listen for the symptoms. Too often stress is dealt with too late. Listen to your employees when they're expressing themselves and watch for signs of unhappiness or anxiety. When these signs appear, be ready to help them solve the problems. Don't lazily and silently respond with thoughts like "it will pass," or "they better just get it together!" It may take time on your part but that's what being a manager means. Taking time means you care. If you don't catch the symptoms as they arise, you'll still be hearing all about them just like too many other managers . . . during employee exit interviews. Then you've missed your chance. It's a choice between preventive maintenance and holding out for a complete breakdown. The decision is yours.

## RECOMMENDED RESOURCES ON STRESS MANAGEMENT
- **Beat Stress with Strength;**
  *A Survival Guide for Work and Life*
  By: Stephanie Spera and Sandra Lanto (book)
- **Catch Fire**; *A Seven-Step Program to Ignite Energy, Defuse Stress and Power Boost Your Career*
  By Peter McLaughlin (book)

- **Don't Sweat It!**
  *Richard Carlson's Low Stress Strategies for Success*
  By Richard Carlson (audio)
- **Freeze Frame**; *One Minute Stress Management:*
  *A Scientifically Proven Technique for Clear Decision*
  *Making and Improved Health*
  By Doc Lew Childre (book)
- **Self Discipline and Emotional Control;**
  *How to Stay Calm and Productive Under Pressure*
  By Tom Miller (audio or video)
- **Stress Management for Professionals;**
  *Staying Balanced Under Pressure*
  By Roger Mellott (audio or video)
- **Stress Skills for Turbulent Times;**
  *How to Manage the Multiple Demands*
  *Facing Today's Working Woman*
  By Roger Mellott (audio)

For articles on stress management related to telemarketing, contact industry publications such as the magazines and journals listed below and request a list of past articles on this subject. You can select the articles you want, usually for a nominal fee. Believe me, it's worth it.

- *Call Center Magazine* (215-355-2886)
- *Teleprofessional* (319-235-4473)
- *Sales and Marketing Strategies & News* (800-435-2937)
- *Selling Power* (800-752-7355)

# A Final Thought by Dave Worman

I have a final thought regarding the contents of this book but certainly not about the subject of non-monetary motivation. This subject will never have a final thought because in my eyes it will remain one of the most influential factors in raising performance and reducing the turnover of our telephone professionals and employees across most industries. And on that note, let me assure you that this entire book is built not on theory, guesswork or probability, but on fact. The ideas, programs, contests and suggestions in every chapter are drawn from real circumstances in my own career in this wonderful business of ours. With every page I would find myself celebrating my past achievements, laughing at unforgettable memories and mentally bleeding during my flashbacks of managerial mistakes. Above all I often found myself enthusiastic and excited about what can and will happen in your environments as you turn some of these pages into human reality. Too optimistic, you say? Remember that I already know the outcome. I've been there. I am there. At some time in my telesales management career I have used every one of the ideas that fill every one of these chapters. Many of these ideas are alive and well in my current environment. And you can rest assured that I will continue to use as many of them as possible in my everyday professional life.

What about you? Will you continue to do what you've always done and continue to get what you've always gotten? Or will you challenge yourself to make the time and exert the energy to implement some of the ideas in this book that I guarantee will produce higher levels of divisional and corporate success by more motivated employees? You may remember when Joe

Namath used this chancy word at the 1969 Super Bowl? He *guaranteed* that his New York Jets would beat the highly favored Baltimore Colts in Super Bowl III. While I may not be as cool as Broadway Joe, I do have the same amount of confidence in your success as Namath had in his own team to guarantee you higher performance, productivity, morale, loyalty and job dedication.

As always, I am available to assist you and your organization in setting up incentive programs, training procedures and overall motivational solutions. It's always fun to roll up my sleeves with telesales management teams across the continent and watch the excitement spread and the positive results explode. If you would be interested in this kind of assistance or even a simple presentation, let's talk about it. Please give me a call at home at (815) 434-6579 or send email to DWorman@Reliable.com.

Finally, I will leave you with the very same thought I share whenever I autograph one of my books. *Thanks for your interest and remember enthusiasm is contagious!* Use this book to create an epidemic of enthusiasm in your environment. When you do, get ready to deal with an epidemic of success.

# More Management, Motivational, and Telesales Resources You Can Order Right Now

☐ *"Motivating With Sales Contests : Motivating Your Telephone Professionals With Contests That Produce Record-Breaking Results, Including 79 Contests You Can Use Right Now!*
### By Dave Worman
Get Dave's first book, showing you everything you need to know to run morale-enhancing, sales-boosting, turnover-reducing contests. Plus you get 79 actual, tested and proven sales contests explained in detail you can run immediately! $29 (+3.50 shipping)

☐ *"Telephone Sales Management and Motivation Made Easy—With 50 Sales Contests You Can Use Immediately"*
By Valerie Sloane and Theresa Arvizo Jackson
If you're like most managers, there's simply not enough time to regularly come up with fresh, useable ideas that keep your salespeople motivated and producing at high levels. This 166-page paperback is jammed with proven ideas you can use right now to make your job easier, while creating a fun environment that motivates your reps to close more sales, including 50 more contests you can run. $19.95 ($3.50 shipping)

☐ **"The Successful Sales Manager's Guide to Business-to-Business Telephone Sales--Everything You Need to Start, Reposition, and Manage a Telesales Department"**
By Lee Van Vechten
In this massive 300+ page resource, you have the step-by-step guidelines for starting (or repositioning) and running a successful telephone sales operation. This is a complete how-to guide for managers, giving you proven, field-tested strategic and tactical information you will use to avoid costly mistakes, and run your telephone sales operation like a well-oiled, money making machine. Regardless of whether you're a veteran telephone sales manager, or just looking to start up an inside sales department, you'll have the benefit of Lee VanVechten's 37+ years of experience in telemarketing sales, management, and consulting. Businesses gladly pay thousands of dollars to hire Lee personally for his expertise, and it makes them hundreds of thousands, and in many cases, millions of dollars. $79 ($5 shipping)

# To Order Any of These Items
1. Mail your check, U.S. funds only, to Business By Phone, 13254 Stevens St., Omaha, NE, 68137.
2. Call us at 1-800-326-7721.
3. Fax your order with credit card number to (402)896-3353.
4. Order online at www.businessbyphone.com

# Here Are Other Resources You Can Get Right Now to Help You Manage, Motivate, and SELL!

## Go to Our Website for Lots of FREE Telesales Tips, Special Offers, and Other Resources to Help You
## www.businessbyphone.com

### Have Information In Seconds With Business By Phone's Fax-Back Service

You can have detailed descriptions of plenty of sales-building products in your hands as soon as you want. Go the handset of your fax machine, call (402)896-9877, listen for the prompts, press "1," and follow the instructions. When asked, press "101" as the document you'd like. This is our Fax Information Directory listing all of the brochures and samples available to you by return fax. Receive this document, pick the additional information you'd like, then call again to receive your choices. Or, simply use the document numbers below to make your selections.

### FREE! "The TelE-Sales Hot Tips of the Week" Newsletter

Each week you will have sales tips and words of motivation from Art Sobczak e-mailed to your desk, free! Sign up by e-mailing to **arts @businessbyphone.com** with "join" in the subject line, or go to **www.businessbyphone.com** and sign up yourself. Plus, you will get a free special report for simply sigining up.

### Get a FREE Subscription to the Business By Phone Catalog of Tapes, Books, Telesales Rep College Seminars, Other Training Materials

Call our offices at 1-800-326-7721.

### The Telesales Rep College Two-Day Training Workshops

Throughout the year Art personally delivers 8-10 public training programs across the U.S., covering every step of the professional telesales call. Valuable for rookies and veterarns alike, you'll leave energized, armed with new ideas to deploy right away to grab more business on your very next call. Only 25 participants accepted per session.Call 1-800-326-7721 for the current schedule, or select Fax Information Document 108.

# Get More Copies of This Book, and Dave's Other Book, "Motivating With Sales Contests"

To get additional copies of this book, and/or Dave's first book, "Motivating With Sales Contests," photocopy or remove this form, or call, fax, or e-mail us with the necessary information. *(Inquire about quantity discounts. Also, bookstore and dealer inquiries welcome.)*

☐ ___copies of "Motivating Without Money," @ $29.95 (+$3.50 shipping U.S., $7 foreign, US funds)

☐ ___copies of **"Motivating With Sales Contests"** @ $29 (+$3.50 shipping U.S., $7 foreign, US funds)

### *Special Set Pricing Discount!*

☐ Save! Get both books for only $49.00. (+$6 shipping U.S., $10 foreign, US funds) Send ____ sets.

**Name**_____

**Company**_____

**Address**_____

**City**_____**State**_____**Zip Code**_____

**Phone**_____

**Fax**_____


## Method of Payment

☐ Visa/MC/AMEX/Discover

   #_____

   sig._____exp._____

☐ Check /Money Order Enclosed *(U.S. Funds Only)*


## Ways to Order

- **Phone your order to 1-800-326-7721, or (402)895-9399.**
- **Fax your order to (402)896-3353.**
- **Mail your order to Business By Phone,**
     **13254 Stevens St., Omaha, NE, 68137.**
- **E-Mail your order to orders@businessbyphone.com.**
- **Order online at www.businessbyphone.com.**